# Researching for Television and Radio

*Researching for Television and Radio* is an essential guide to working as a researcher in the television and radio industries. It explains the stages of programme making, identifies the main areas of production, details the important role of the researcher and explores key areas of the job.

*Researching for Television and Radio* offers practical advice and instruction on technical, ethical and legal issues which affect researchers. Beginning with suggestions on how to think up programme ideas and devise treatments, through to general research methods and techniques, and guidance on filming and recording on location and abroad, it uses real examples of good and bad practice from the industry. Written by an experienced researcher and producer, *Researching for Radio and Television* includes:

- tips on finding contributors from contestants and audiences to experts and specialists

- advice on filming, video recording and using music

- how to find photographs, pictures and film clips

- a discussion of risk assessment, codes of conduct, ethical behaviour and safety issues

- a guide to essential directories and reference works

- a glossary of television and radio terms, further reading and a list of helpful websites.

**Adèle Emm** teaches at Hopwood Hall College in Manchester. She has worked in film-editing at the BBC, as a freelance researcher at Thames and Tyne Tees Television, and staff researcher and producer at Granada.

# Media Skills

Series Editor: Richard Keeble, City University, London
Series Advisers: Wynford Hicks and Jenny McKay

The *Media Skills* series provides a concise and thorough introduction to a rapidly changing media landscape. Each book is written by media and journalism lecturers or experienced professionals and is a key resource for a particular industry. Offering helpful advice and information and using practical examples from print, broadcast and digital media, as well as discussing ethical and regulatory issues, *Media Skills* books are essential guides for students and media professionals.

Also in this series:

**English for Journalists, 2nd edition**
*Wynford Hicks*

**Writing for Journalists**
*Wynford Hicks with Sally Adams and Harriett Gilbert*

**Interviewing for Radio**
*Jim Beaman*

**Producing for the Web**
*Jason Whittaker*

**Ethics for Journalists**
*Richard Keeble*

**Scriptwriting for the Screen**
*Charlie Moritz*

**Interviewing for Journalists**
*Sally Adams, with an introduction and additional material by Wynford Hicks*

**Reporting for Journalists**
*Chris Frost*

Find more details of current *Media Skills* books and forthcoming titles at
**www.producing.routledge.com**

# Researching for
# Television and Radio

Adèle Emm

LONDON AND NEW YORK

# For Pasqualle

First published 2002
by Routledge
11 New Fetter Lane, London EC4P 4EE

Simultaneously published in the USA and Canada
by Routledge
29 West 35th Street, New York, NY 10001

*Routledge is an imprint of the Taylor & Francis Group*

© 2002 Adèle Emm

Typeset in Goudy Old Style and Syntax by Wearset Ltd, Boldon, Tyne and Wear
Printed and bound in Great Britain by Biddles Ltd, Guildford and King's Lynn

*British Library Cataloguing in Publication Data*
A catalogue record for this book is available from the British Library

*Library of Congress Cataloging in Publication Data*
Emm, Adèle, 1953–
    Researching for television and radio / Adèle Emm.
        p. cm. — (Media skills)
    Includes bibliographical references and index.
        1. Television—Production and direction—Vocational guidance—Great Britain. 2.
    Radio—Production and direction—Vocational guidance—Great Britain. I. Title. II.
        Series.
    PN1992.75 E48 2001
    791.44'902'93—dc21

                                                                                2001019894

    ISBN 0-415-24387-4 (alk. paper)
    ISBN 0-415-24388-2 (pbk. : alk. paper)

# Contents

# Acknowledgements

BBC Television for reproducing extracts from their Producer's Guidelines.
Broadcasting Standards Commission for reproducing extracts from their codes.
Independent Television Commission for permission to reproduce part of their Programme Codes.
The Radio Authority for permission to reproduce part of their Programme Code.
The Health and Safety Executive.
Ro Barratt, producer and writer.
Shazna Begum, researcher, BBC.
Violet Berlin.
Steven Blyth, Stockport Council Elections Office.
Chris Cowey, Executive Producer, *Top of the Pops*, BBC.
Sharon Dean, Head of Licensing Services, MCPS.
Bob Dickinson, BBC radio producer, for helping me with Chapter 10.
Dawn Evans, Film and Television Commission, North West.
Ken Everett, Health and Safety Officer, Granada TV.
Jacquie Farnham, researcher, BBC.
Wendy Franks, Equity, for information from the Equity Television Agreements 2000.
John Fleming.
Roy Greener and the Reader Admissions Office at the British Library.
Bill Kerr, Musicians Union, for helping me with Chapter 7.
ITN Archive.
Sheila McCormick, floor manager.
Luke McKernen, Head of Information, British Universities Film and Video Council.
Glen Marks, Library Manager, Rex Features Picture Agency.
Christine Mummery, Manchester Council Education Welfare Office.
Charlotte Ross, *Top of the Pops* researcher, BBC.

Don Trafford, TV production manager, for vetting the content of Chapters 8 and 9.

Nick Tyrrell for support, reading the hard parts of the manuscript and just being there.

# Disclaimer

A lot of care has been taken in researching this book but certain issues such as copyright are extremely complicated. Readers should be aware that specialists such as in-house experts or copyright lawyers should be consulted whenever possible. The book is devised to offer advice on a number of issues but the author and publishers cannot accept responsibility for accidents or other health and safety issues.

# Introduction

What you do as a researcher depends very much on what you make of the job, the effort you put into it and the programme you work on. It has never been and never will be 9 to 5, and it has never been a doddle. But it can be the most amazing fun and it should be incredibly rewarding.

This book is designed as a handbook to point out potential pitfalls so that the media professional is aware beforehand of anything outrageous – and expensive – that might occur. It is not possible to anticipate all contingencies, but many professionals working in the industry today have read the manuscript and added their own helpful pointers.

The chapter titles speak for themselves. Readers are not expected to begin at the beginning and work through, although the book can be read in this way. The Glossary and List of Abbreviations cover more than is specifically mentioned in this book.

For those working in radio, many of the challenges faced are the same as for their television counterparts and it is common for researchers to migrate across the media. Although Chapter 10 is specifically aimed at the radio researcher, Chapters 2, 3, 4, 11 and 12 are also relevant, as are the Appendices. The use of music is far simpler in radio so a cursory glance at Chapter 7 should suffice.

Enjoy yourself and your job.

Adèle Emm

# 1
# What is a researcher?

A researcher is the person whose name comes third last in the credits before the director and the producer.

In a sitcom, a researcher is portrayed as an intense, worried-looking young person with a *yah* accent and a clipboard stapled to her trendy chest. And it *is* a her, because the trendy young male researcher has been promoted to the intense, trendy young producer with his feet on the desk barking orders. Recognise the stereotype?

Put it out of your mind. The researcher is the king pin gopher, the bottom rung of the production ladder but a job in its own right. A police constable may never make it to a sergeant and a researcher may never make it further up the production ladder but, because of the very nature of the job, this shouldn't matter.

The experienced media researcher has two mottoes:

- 'Give me a phone and I can find you anything.'

- 'The impossible I can do now, a miracle takes a little longer.'

I shall start by describing the personal attributes of a researcher. This is the job description you won't read in the advertisement.

A researcher is/has:

- well educated and informed with interests in a wide variety of subjects; a whizz at *Trivial Pursuits*;

- curious and with the ability to ask pertinent questions and sound convincing even when they know nothing about the subject. By the end of the project, they are an expert. The get-out-of-jail-free is to admit to Professor Whatnot right at the beginning that they haven't a clue about the politics of Papua New Guinea but he is the expert and . . .;

- a good listener with the ability to précis accurately and take good notes;

- an excellent memory;

- hard working. The hours can be appalling; a 105-hour week non-stop for three weeks including weekends is not unusual. Yes, the European Union Social Chapter limits hours to a 48-hour week but middle management is so far exempt;

- fit, healthy, self-starter, assertive, reliable and responsible;

- excellent organisational and administrative skills;

- able to get on with and like people. All people. Rudyard Kipling's *If* sums it up. If you know to what I am referring and have looked it up, you are well on the way;

- meticulous and gives attention to detail;

- good computer skills, including fast typing;

- a facility with language as they often write voiceovers, links and narration;

- a sense of humour (for all those puns) and the ability to get to the nub of an issue in as few words as possible. Television and radio are verbal media and, depending on the production, scripts should read like something you'd say, not a report you'd hand to your accountant. On the other hand, if you are writing for current affairs and political programmes the script should sound like the voice of authority;

- the essential social skills of drinking late into the night, partying until dawn and being back on location bright eyed and bushy tailed at 7 a.m.

As for what the researcher actually does; that is the million dollar question. Depending on the type of production and the size of the team, it is a pivotal position crossing many demarcation lines.

I'll start by explaining the stages of programme making from pre-production through to transmission, giving a thumbnail description of the main jobs in television (see Chapter 10 for radio) and those which crossover with research. There are plenty of jobs I haven't listed and, for reasons of brevity, this is not an exhaustive job specification for each role.

## PRE-PRODUCTION

This is the commissioning, planning and organising of the programme up to the actual shoot. During pre-production, the set is devised and built, the costumes designed, hired or made, the contestants and actors auditioned, special effects designed and produced and the programme planned in detail bearing in mind that, as good ideas crop up, the production is inevitably changed.

Pre-production takes an inordinate length of time. A feature film or historical drama may be in pre-production for several years. However, the escalating use of accountants results in squeezed budgets and increasingly tight pre-production schedules.

The first person assigned to a production, often because it is his/her idea, is the producer, closely followed by the researcher and director.

*Producer:*   in overall charge; responsible for editorial and budgetary control and can hire-and-fire personnel including . . .

*Director:*   has overall responsibility for the visuals – and more . . .

*Researcher:*   read this book!

*Scriptwriter:*   mainly drama, sitcoms and so on, occasionally employed to write banter for Light Entertainment.

*Assistant producer* (occasionally Associate Producer):   one up from a Senior Researcher, second in command to the Producer and often with responsibility for overseeing the budget. In the BBC, may direct studio.

*Associate producer:*   in ITV is usually a consultant role with skills specific to the programme.

*Production/Location manager:*   organises large productions in regard to hiring crews, organising hotels, catering and transport, hiring equipment. The Production Manager checks the budget on a day-to-day basis.

*Production Assistant or PA:*   (in 99 per cent of cases female) types the scripts, running orders, props lists, pays expenses from a float, times and cues studio, completes copyright return forms and cue sheets. On location, acts as continuity, checking props and action are consistent between scenes.

*Assistant director* (also known as First Assistant Director or 1st AD – employed on large location productions only): ensures all actors, crewmembers and facilities are on set at the right time. Organises shooting schedules. In feature film shoots acts as 2nd Unit Director (i.e. for battle scenes). In a TV studio, the 1st AD is known as the *floor manager*.

Production manager's, location manager's and assistant director's jobs often overlap depending on the size and requirements of the production.

## Design Departments

*Set/Production designer:*   responsible for the design of the set both on location and in studio.

*Graphics department:*   responsible for graphics including titles.

*Props buyer, props department, stage crew:*   the *props buyer* locates, buys or hires props; *the props department* places them on set, *the stage crew* moves sets and large furniture. These are under the jurisdiction of the set designer.

*Costume designer:*   designs, buys, hires the costumes; is in charge of the costume/wardrobe assistants who act as dressers to the actors or contestants.

*Makeup designer:*   designs the makeup including hair; is in charge of the makeup assistants who apply basic and uncomplicated makeup.

All of the above liaise with the director.

## PRODUCTION

This is when the programme is recorded on location or in a studio.

Feature films expect to shoot the equivalent of $1\frac{1}{2}$ minutes of screen time a day; in other words a feature film shoot usually lasts ten to sixteen weeks or more depending on the overall length and the budget. Television drama, on the other hand, shoots an hour's drama over eleven days or less if possible. Soaps such as *Coronation Street* record four half-hour episodes a week, more when working towards the Christmas break or for a special.

Ten years ago, one quiz episode was recorded a day but today, up to four are recorded. Why? The same number of studio crew are required in one day to make four shows as are to make one. Simple.

Chat shows and daytime current affairs like *The Time, The Place* and *Kilroy* are usually transmitted live.

Others are recorded *as live*. 'As live' means the programme is taped in real time but pre-recorded a few hours or a day before. There are several reasons for this: a common one being the tx (transmission) time is unsociable (a bank holiday, 3 a.m.) and costs a fortune in wages. The benefit of recording as live is that, although each take is 'for real', should there be any serious faults (technical or editorial) the take can be rewound and re-recorded. There is no editing on an 'as live' programme.

A daily *live* programme such as *This Morning* with Judy Finnigan and Richard Madeley has a separate production team assigned to Monday or Tuesday and throughout the week. Effectively, once the pre-production period is over (perhaps as little as a month setting up pre-recorded items), the team works a rolling schedule culminating in their day's programme. Programmes such as *The Time, The Place* and *Kilroy* work on the same principle with several teams working on a two- or three-week rota.

Here pre-production merges into production. Imagine being on week 4 of a 16-episode local fashion show. The first three programmes have been transmitted, episode 4 is in editing, episode 5 onwards is being shot but no-one has more than the vaguest idea of the content of programme 12 onwards. This happens. Depending on one's attitude, it's very stressful or the most adrenaline-boosting roller coaster ever.

Pre-production personnel are still involved.

## Camera department (in hierarchy order)

*Director of photography/cinematographer:*    (large shoots only) at the pinnacle of his (at the time of writing there are virtually no women at this level) career and able to realise the concept and atmosphere onto the screen via lighting, camera angles and movement.

*Lighting cameraman:*    a day-to-day cameraman who lights small productions; often acts as focus puller or camera operator on larger shoots.

*Focus puller:*    pulls focus on complex cameras for complicated shots.

*Camera operator:*    operates the camera.

*Camera assistant:*    helps carry the equipment, ensures the batteries are fully charged, keeps a record of the camera shots, cable bashes when required (ensures the cables are not trailing on the floor behind the cameraman).

*Clapper/Loader:*    operates the clapper board and keeps it up to date as well as loading the film into the magazines (film mags).

On small shoots, for instance a news item, there may only be a camera operator. The camera assistant and clapper loader is often the same person.

## Electrical department

*Electricians or sparks:*    responsible for rigging the lights and power supplies (gaffers and best boys are in charge and second-in-command of this department).

*Rigger/Drivers:*    drive the transport, help carry the equipment and set up tracks for tracking (moving) shots.

Only on the very largest of shoots will all of the above be present.

## Sound department

*Sound recordist:*   records and mixes sound on location and in studio. Often specialises in either post-production or production.

*Sound assistant:*   helps fix on microphones and acts as . . .

*Boom swinger:*   holds the boom mic (a mic attached to a long pole to be as near as possible to the speaker with the operator out of shot) in the optimum position for the best sound.

*Dubbing mixer:*   post-production only. Mixes the sounds together for a cohesive sound track.

## Studio production

Cameramen, sound recordists, stage, props and sparks as above.

*Vision mixer:*   sits in the studio control room (box or gallery depending on local jargon) and works with the director selecting and mixing the shots in a multi-camera set up.

*Floor manager:*   in charge of the studio floor including health and safety issues.

*Technical supervisor (TS):*   responsible for the technical side of the studio including cameras, sound and recording equipment.

## POST-PRODUCTION

Once filming is over, it is technically in post-production. This is when editing takes place (where the shots are put in the correct order and mistakes cut out), special effects added, sound re-recorded and mixed (dubbed) and a master edit produced.

For live programmes, there is no post-production, although the programme will be recorded whilst being transmitted.

*Editors:*   edit the rushes (uncut footage straight from the camera).

*Sound editors:*   a film or video has several 'layers' of sound and sound editors compile and edit the sound tracks.

## TX (TRANSMISSION)

This is when the programme goes out on air.

## The researcher's role

Researchers work on a variety of programmes, such as:

- documentaries and documentary series/docu-soaps/infotainment;

- light entertainment/quizzes/game shows;

- music;

- sport;

- children's programmes;

- magazine/day time/chat shows;

- news and current affairs (although these prefer to employ journalists);

- drama (but few dramas employ researchers as such).

This is what researchers do:

- suggest ideas;

- suggest new treatments;

- find contributors, audition and interview them and 'mind' them in studio or on location (celebrities, experts, MPs, contestants, documentary subjects);

- supervise and organise the personal props of programme contributors;

- pay expenses to contributors;

- check the spelling of contributors' names;

- check facts;

- find statistics and confirm their accuracy;

- set and verify quiz questions and act as scorekeepers;

- organise hotels, restaurants, travel arrangements for self, contributors and crews;

- book specialist equipment in consultation with film crews;

- find props, prizes and costumes;

- find locations and go on recces (short for 'reconnaissance', see Chapter 8);

- suggest atmospheric music;

- research, direct, shoot and edit short inserts for television;

- supervise editing including devising paper edits (the cutting order or the EDL, edit decision list);

- research, direct, record and edit sound packages for radio and organise ISDN lines;

- act as an on-screen reporter on short items;

- write links, voiceovers, narrations;

- organise photographic shoots;

- find film clips, photographs and pictures and organise their satellite links and transfer from different formats.

Many of these mirror other production roles but the larger and more prestigious the programme and the larger the budget, the less likely the researcher will take on some of the responsibilities of the list above. However, on cable and satellite stations, where the budget is virtually non-existent, the researcher may do everything from research, shoot, edit and dance the polka at the same time. All for £10,000 a year. And why would anyone be mug enough to research, direct, produce, shoot and edit a satellite station's entire output? For the experience. Because they have direct editorial control. Because they are desperate for a job in the industry. Someone else will do it for less and it's a good place to begin a career.

Generally speaking, however, the researcher is responsible for offering ideas, finding contributors and suggesting angles by which a pretty ordinary idea can be recorded in an unusual, novel and interesting way.

In the words of Chris Cowey, the Executive Producer of *Top of the Pops*, a researcher needs the 4 I's:

Innovation. Imagination. Intelligence. Integrity.

He added that a good researcher is extremely hard to find and harder to keep because, in this day and age where a researcher's job is not regarded as a be all and end all, either they are poached by other programmes or they become a producer.

The beauty of working as a researcher is that no two jobs are ever the same. Researchers may find themselves working for six months on a chat show followed by a music programme and then a year's contract on current affairs where a different subject is tackled each week.

In a nutshell, a researcher is a jack-of-all-trades with opportunities to specialise in their preferred genre depending on their background and interest.

## A BRIEF NOTE ABOUT CONTRACTS

Until the 1990 Broadcasting Act, a large number of jobs in radio and television were permanent 'staff' jobs in which an employee worked for the same company until they retired or found a job elsewhere. Since then, the majority of jobs in film, television and radio are short fixed-term contracts usually of a few months' duration.

Production personnel, including researchers, cannot assume that any fixed-term contract will be renewed and they must expect to work where a job is available. Inevitably, this means moving frequently. The majority of work is in London and many media professionals resent moving south with its exorbitant house prices and the inherent problems of short-term contracts. Manchester, Leeds, Birmingham, Nottingham, Southampton, Bristol and Glasgow are also large media centres.

Most media newcomers obtain their first job at independent production houses and in cable television. These tend to be based in cities, although cable stations are now setting up in larger towns. Contracts and pay are short and low.

Radio stations are, by their nature, more regional and localised. Competition for jobs is less fierce than for television but fierce enough! On the whole, for most independent radio stations, there are fewer jobs in production and most people work in marketing and promotions.

The downside of short-term contracts is the instability. The upside is that, if you find routine tedious and savour change and new challenges, this is perfect.

## A NOTE ON ETHICS

A global and dangerous statement is that a producer often wants what is impossible. The researcher is in the unfortunate position of having to provide something the producer doesn't know they want until they see it. This sounds harsh but is reality and can result in ethically questionable products.

* In December 1998, Carlton Television was fined £2 million by the ITC for setting up drug runners in a *Cutting Edge* documentary on the Columbian drug trade.

* In 1999, Nottingham Council took Channel 4 and October Films to court for paying schoolchildren to sit in doorways and act as prostitutes whilst the cameras rolled.

* *Vanessa* and *Trisha* were discredited for fake guests. The *Vanessa* show was axed in June 1999. *The Jerry Springer Show* from the USA has been revealed for winding up its guests until they 'fight' on set.

As production schedules tighten to save money, the researcher has less time to supply a controversial guest with an outspoken, outrageous viewpoint. If a guest has come up with the goods before, do you use them again? Even if their face has appeared on three different talk shows with a different spin on each? Do you pay them a fee for something they neither care in nor believe?

The answer, of course, is *no* and yet the researcher has to deliver at all costs or their contract isn't renewed. Yet if the programme is axed because of fixing, the researcher has lost their job anyway.

In May 1999, The British Film Institute published a survey in which producers blamed cost cutting for the number of fakes. The BFI report said, 'bowing to pressures for exciting and entertaining programmes had become almost habitual within factual programming' (British Film Institute's *Television Industry Tracking Survey*, May 24, 1999).

After the debacle of *Vanessa*, the BBC issued guidelines whereby all guests on factual programmes must sign an honesty declaration exonerating the production team should the guest prove fraudulent. This cannot condone the harassed researcher cutting corners and taking the easy way out.

## CULPABILITY AND RECRIMINATION?

Does it matter if the responsibility lies with you or the producer? If the producer overrides what you have provided in all good faith, and if you have acted ethically, then ultimately it is the producer's responsibility. Just ensure you have proof to cover your own back when the blame is apportioned.

The researcher's job involves long hours, is extraordinarily hard and stressful but exciting, satisfying and fulfilling. It's like the old anti-army joke; a researcher gets the chance to go to many places, meet both influential and ordinary people – and shoot them. On video.

## FURTHER READING

Chater, Kathy, *Production Research, An Introduction*, Focal Press, 1998.
Hart, Colin, *Television Programme Making*, Focal Press, 1999.
Holland, Patricia, *The Television Handbook*, Routledge, 2nd edn, 2000.
Keeble, Richard, *Ethics for Journalists*, Routledge, 2001.
McLeish, Robert, *Radio Production*, Focal Press, 4th edn, 1999.
Wilby, Pete and Conroy, Andy, *The Radio Handbook*, Routledge, 1994.
Watts, Harris, *On Camera, Essential Know-how for Programme Makers*, Aavo, revised 1997.

# 2
# Ideas

There are no new ideas in television; everything has been done before. Your task is to find a different way of doing it, to find a new angle, to give it a new treatment.

With hundreds of channels of television on air 24 hours a day and hundreds of programme hours to fill, anyone who can whistle up novel, interesting, exciting, sexy ideas will never find themselves out of work. But where do these ideas come from?

This is the hardest part of any researcher's job. Some people have the knack of being inventive and creative. Others work at it. I remember talking to a colleague about a one-minute package for the Samaritans for a television day-long charity appeal. 'Just have a BCU (big close up) of a ringing phone,' he replied. 'And don't answer it.' Simple, wonderfully effective and cheap.

## COPYRIGHTING IDEAS

Ideas in general cannot be copyrighted. Formats can, and some television companies, notably those producing game and quiz shows, buy and sell formats. One of the most famous court cases involving copyright was when Hughie Green, the presenter of *Opportunity Knocks*, sued a New Zealand TV company for producing a similar amateur talent contest. He lost the case because the *scripts* were not deemed close enough to have infringed the format.

Media people are unprincipled enough to pinch ideas and pass them off as their own, resulting in job interviewees or colleagues in a pub refusing to divulge their precious ideas in case it is screened with somebody else's credit or the appointment goes elsewhere. At the job interview, this strategy misfires if the second best ideas are mediocre.

## EXCLUSIVITY

If creativity and good ideas are so difficult, is it surprising that television (radio less so) constantly demands the scoop, the first airing of a new video, the exclusive interview, the hitherto unseen footage?

There are no easy answers but there *are* strategies. To have ideas, you must be interested and open to everything. Television is so all-consuming, it is easy to lose sight of what is going on around you simply because you are too busy making programmes.

## KEEP UP TO DATE AND BE INFORMED

If a reply to an interview question, 'And what are your hobbies?' is 'Erm, I haven't any,' there is a serious problem. Job applicants are commonly turned down because of a lack of outside interests. People with diverse interests, no matter how unusual or anorakish, are more creative with more to draw on. The more they do, even if it isn't television or radio experience, the more likely they are to have ideas.

It is vital to know what is going on in the world. Read magazines such as *Smash Hits, Loaded, OK* and *Woman*. Even the *Beano*. The *Sun* won't tax your brain but you'll know what the editor thinks the public wants. Don't forget the broadsheets: *The Times, Guardian* and *Daily Telegraph*. Know the issues of the moment and keep up with them. Who's in? Who's out? Who wants to be in? Who are the movers and shakers in politics, the arts and the business world? What's on at the cinema but, crucially, what is filmed today for distribution next year? And who is tipped for the big time?

You can never know too much, however trivial and irrelevant it may appear. As your life changes, go with it. After having her family, Esther Rantzen used her experience to make programmes about birth, babies and children's issues. After I had my daughter, I worked on similar programmes. The tragedy of this anecdote is that, because so few women in television juggle a career with bringing up children and as most other women around me were single and childless, by merely giving birth I became an expert.

## IDEA SOURCES

### Brainstorming

Even something as banal as the British obsession with weather can become a valid topic. The method of brainstorming involves thinking round the subject in as silly or serious way as you can. The rules are simple. Nobody laughs and all suggestions are jotted down. All sorts of treatments will crop up and many can be adapted to suit a particular programme.

Weather forecasting by folklore for a lifestyle programme. Cue a dotty expert who foretells a tsunami in Tijuana because the daffodil in his garden faces east. Include the famous clip when Michael Fish got it wrong.

Turn the idea around and you get a programme about how not to get flu during winter – cue a phone-in of granny's fail-safe way of keeping the bugs away by wearing mustard plasters on her corns.

In a children's programme like *Blue Peter*, the weather becomes 'infotainment', Canadian Inuit children surviving extreme conditions with, of course, location filming.

Other examples might be 'The World's Worst Ten Meteorological Disasters' to 'Why Take Aspirin For a Cold?' and the celebrity chat on 'How I Nearly Died of Flu!'

## Treatments

A treatment is how the item is tackled. Take the closing of the Common Cold Centre in Salisbury; for the national news, its treatment is a serious interview with an eminent professor and the Minister for Health. Regional news might tackle the angle of job losses, interviewing employees and the local MP. *Tomorrow's World* focuses on the scientific and medical angle of the common cold and *This Morning* might, to use a previous idea, include a light-hearted phone in on old wives' cures. The same story but a different audience and a different treatment, in studio or location, some more humorous whilst others are serious.

One of the best treatments I saw recently was for a children's animal programme. The item was about the bee dance where bees waggle their bottoms to indicate to other bees where to find the pollen. This could have been tedious – a voice over stock shots of bees and flowers. Instead it was a musical montage with two presenters dressed in dirty macs greeting each other in a large meadow. Removing their coats to music, they revealed dinner jacket and tails and waltzed 1930s style through the flowers accompanied only by sound effects and comic book bubble box captions. Brilliant.

## The futures desk

In newspaper offices and TV and radio station newsrooms, the futures desk keeps a diary on what is happening over the next few months.

Sports events are fixed months, often years, in advance. Everyone knows when and where the next Olympic games will be staged. Wimbledon is held the last week of June and the first week of July. The Football Association draws the fixtures and announces the dates well in advance. Other sporting information is sent by the governing bodies to the futures desk in the form of press releases and these are entered into the futures diary.

Events such as Christmas, Hallowe'en and Easter are annual. Daytime television, children's shows and lifestyle programmes base one if not several programmes on these themes because it is in the viewer's agenda already and, frankly, because it is easy. How often has *Blue Peter* made variations of Advent calendars and Easter bunnies?

The Queen's birthday, Crufts Dog Show and Wimbledon are regular items. Why? Because everyone knows when they take place and therefore they become ideas; the what-is-being-worn-at-Ascot-this-year, the youngest-person-entering-a-dog-in-the-show, the how-to-improve-your-tennis approach.

If you can think of ingenious ideas and treatments, apply for a job.

## Press releases

Press releases are brief information leaflets usually one side long giving the main points of an approaching event. They are sent out by an organisation wanting publicity, preferably free, to national and local newspaper offices, national and local radio stations and television stations with the intention of it being used as newspaper articles, or television and radio items.

Examples of when press releases may be sent out are:

- the publication date of the latest novel by a blockbusting writer;
- the opening of a new play;
- special awareness health days (e.g. no smoking or breast cancer);
- changes in government policy;
- changes in social security payments;
- the Royal Mail's new postal charges or stamp designs;
- a local Brownie pack advertising a bravery award;
- a company expanding employment;
- a school or college where a student has achieved something special;
- a local sporting event;
- the opening of a children's hospice;
- a local street carnival;
- a pop group signing records in a high street store.

In many cases, the press release is advertising something low key but, although it isn't a huge occasion, it may catch the eye of the local radio station researcher or become a two- or three-minute item in a regional news programme.

Often a press release may have a few words changed and appear almost in its original form as an article in a local newspaper – free publicity indeed and exactly what the writer of the press release intended.

In some cases, for instance a pop group's appearance at a record shop, the press release initiates a media event and the shop's promoters, the record company and the group's managers all write their own. The police control traffic and fans, stills photographers are hired – and with luck and planning, roll up a complete media circus with local press and television cameras and, hold your breath, national news crews too.

Press releases by their very nature impart the same format although the writing style depends on the source and style of the writer. The information consists of:

* the event;
* the organisers;
* the location;
* general background information: names, ages, the gist;
* when it takes place;
* a contact name and number for further information.

For the television researcher setting up an item from a press release, the first step is to contact the organiser.

## Embargoes

An embargo is occasionally put on a press release. In other words, the organis-ing body requests that the information is released *after* a certain date or time. The recording of the Queen's Christmas Day speech is covered by an embargo clause and, in one famous incident, the *Sun* printed the speech several days early, provoking considerable outrage.

## Personal contacts

Don't underestimate the benefit of your own hobbies and interests. The old maxim exhorting you to write about what you know is good advice. Use your own background as ideas. If your Saturday job was at Tescos, it may throw up an idea for a radio or television topic. It also provides personal contacts and insight, both of which are invaluable. Whenever possible, use them.

A school friend who trampolined for Leicestershire is a minefield of helpful information. One phone call will gain leads on who to speak to at the trampolining club, the governing body and phone number, how much headroom is required (vital in studio) and suggestions of different ways to tackle the item. The 'When I was trampolining, I never saw' – becomes the new angle. The old boys' and girls' network is alive and well in television and radio.

Working in the media hermetically seals you from reality and friends from 'outside' keep you in touch with the world. A simple chat in the pub can produce ideas for a *Generation Game* game to medical documentaries. Keep a handful of index cards in your wallet or handbag and jot them down for brainstorming later.

## Hospitals, police, fire brigade, armed services, local councils, etc.

These organisations commonly use press statements to release information to the media. By their very nature, these groups are the lifeblood of the daily news and are contactable via their Press Office or Public Relations Departments. Up-to-date phone numbers are published in *The Guardian Media Guide*.

However, unless a researcher is working on the news, ideas are rarely initiated from these groups unless you develop an interesting idea from an unusual press release.

The armed forces are often more than willing to work with high-profile LE programmes (except at times of national crisis) and regard media involvement as positive public relations and self-promotion. Any ideas involving the army, navy or air force is well worth exploring. What helps is that, once they have agreed to cooperate, everything works like clockwork with guaranteed professionalism.

## LOCATION OR STUDIO?

It's no good suggesting taking someone to see an acre of rain forest in Belize if the programme is studio based. I once worked on a wish-fulfilment programme with a minimal budget where all wishes had to be fulfilled in studio. Without notifying them of this, the public were asked to send in ideas. Most were greedy and uninspiring along the lines of, 'I want to go first class on the Orient Express' and did not meet the requirements. There was no second series.

This doesn't mean that a location idea can't be adapted for a studio setting although, unless the treatment is brilliant, it can fall flat on its face.

I fell into this trap in my first researcher's job. 'Let's have,' I said enthusiastically, 'indoor fireworks in studio.' Fortunately, I had enough sense to test the idea on camera beforehand. There we were, the producer/director, the head of cameras and the TV company safety officer standing round as a man from the firework company duly brought out some worryingly small fireworks from a worryingly small suitcase. Three minutes later, the politest phrase I heard was 'damp squibs', which is why you rarely see indoor fireworks on television. The River Thames Millennium Wall of Fire had the same effect.

In other words, ideas and their treatment must be appropriate to the programme format but they must also be effective, innovative, imaginative, exciting and visual. Once again, most of those four indispensable I's.

## FURTHER READING

Chater, Kathy, *Production Research, An Introduction*, Focal Press, 1998.
Watts, Harris, *On Camera, Essential Know-how For Programme Makers*, Aavo, revised 1997.

# 3
# General research methods

Media research is nothing like academic research unless a researcher is hired for their specific expertise on, say, archaeology. A huge proportion of media research takes place over the telephone; the rest involves the Internet or going out in the field and many researchers are desk based, never leaving the office. There is little reading of books although referral to source material, directories and the like, is essential.

## PRIMARY RESEARCH

On the whole, TV and radio researchers find themselves involved in first-hand, primary research – meeting people, making phone calls and going on recces. Doing everything from scratch is effectively the media researcher's bread and butter.

## SECONDARY RESEARCH

This is finding source material such as old newspaper reports, watching old documentaries and reading around the subject.

Both primary and secondary research has a role to play; however, for secondary research, someone else has done the original spadework and the secondary resources may include mistakes and personal opinions. Not everything you read in the newspapers or watch on television is true. Whenever possible, secondary research should be verified.

## USING THE TELEPHONE

For some spurious reason, new researchers are telephone-phobic preferring to spend hours seeking an anonymous Internet web page which, once located, doesn't reveal the required information.

There is no replacement for speaking to real people. It irons out ambiguities and gets immediate specific answers. If not, at least you can ask the person on the other end to suggest another contact and give you their number.

If phone phobia is the result of being unsure what to ask, jot down the questions first in note form to prevent the 'parrot fashion' approach that sounds pompous and false. A good phone manner and the ability to prise out answers comes with experience. The more time spent on the phone, the easier and more efficient you are. Boringly, practice does make perfect.

In my experience, I have found that the public believe who you say you are and take you on trust if you phone them first. Paradoxically, turning up on spec has less credibility even when armed with a press pass or ID card. Isn't it annoying when someone ignores you to answer a ringing phone? Yet anyone can claim anything over the telephone. Radio DJ Steve Penk, live on Capital Radio, phoned Tony Blair in Downing Street pretending to be the leader of the Conservative Party, William Hague, and it was some minutes before Tony Blair realised. Incidentally, impersonating someone else is fraud.

## THE PERSONAL APPROACH

It occasionally happens that a researcher needs to go into the field. During the miner's strike, no-one would talk to me over the telephone let alone agree to being filmed. I drove 200 miles north to the picket lines to find someone. Depending on how the rest of the media has treated them, seeing you in person may make them more amenable.

Always be professional, behave politely, sympathetically and impartially to your contacts. As the researcher is often the first contact the general public has with the media, you are the friendly face in a bewildering world and it is common for researchers to end up close friends with their contacts. On the other hand, people may refuse to be filmed because of treatment received at the hands of media 'professionals' in the past.

## INTERVIEWING SKILLS OVER THE PHONE AND FACE-TO-FACE

This section is purely concerned with how to glean information for research purposes and not how to conduct an interview on camera or microphone.

Before you speak to anyone, you need to be sure what you want to achieve. Picking up the phone and pausing when you get through gives the impression of a fool, especially if the person at the other end is extremely busy. Jot down a list of key words beforehand and if, during the course of the conversation, other things spring to mind, jot them down to ask later. Two questions at once, in other words multiple questions, are difficult to answer.

Remember:

- be courteous;

- what do you *need* to know?

- use the familiar questions: Who? What? Where? When? Why? Which? and How?

- what does the crew/producer *need* to know?

- what does the viewer/listener *want* to know?

- listen. Don't do all the talking;

- if they answer your next question before you ask, don't ask it. Merely confirm the gist;

- don't get bogged down taking notes whilst you are talking. Brief notes should suffice;

- if you don't understand, say so. If you want clarification, repeat what they have said in your own words and check they agree;

- confirm essential facts. Get them to spell names and addresses;

- is there anyone else they recommend you to talk to? Can they give a contact number?

- thank them for their time and information;

- write up the notes while you remember.

## NOTE TAKING

Good note-taking skills are essential. Most researchers find the best way of keeping them is in a large, hardback A4 margined and lined notebook. It is an adjunct to the contacts book (explained later, p. 21) and a useful place to jot down names and phone numbers before transferring them into the contacts book. Comments, recce notes and general research can be written here and it is harder to mislay a hardback A4 notebook than scrappy bits of paper.

## STARTING YOUR RESEARCH

Finding the first lead is the hardest part, especially if the topic is something you know nothing about. One of the challenges of the job is its very uncertainty, with researchers working in an area where they have no background whatsoever. Employing uninformed people on the job may appear unprofessional but researchers are highly educated graduates and, for a magazine or current affairs programme, it is impossible to employ someone with an expertise on everything. Specialisation, yes, omniscience, no. I have worked on fly-fishing stories, scrap metal dealing, pig washing, Swedish refuse collection, deep-sea survival techniques and hot air ballooning – none of which I knew anything about until I made the programme. I am no expert on any of them but know considerably more than I did – even if I'd rather not.

Because of time restraints, most preliminary research nowadays takes place over the phone or Internet and often, *all* research is conducted by phone. It is unfortunate, but meeting people prior to recording is a luxury nowadays.

Finding the first lead is a matter of luck, judgement, experience and knowing where to start. Finding someone to talk to in the first place directs you elsewhere and each lead brings further invaluable information. All names and leads should be noted down.

## THE CONTACTS BOOK

The essential tool in any researcher's briefcase is the contacts book. Some researchers keep names and addresses in a large A4-sized address book, preferably hardback and the larger and thicker the better.

Those with a technical bent may prefer a palm-top computer. The advantage of this is, with systematic floppy disk back up or frequent downloading, the mislaying or loss of the palm top is not a total catastrophe. Others use *Outlook* or a similar database system. During the week, the names and addresses are logged into a small notebook with circles ringed around useful names. At the end of the week all useful names are processed into the system and cross-referenced under twenty or so categories making retrieval quick and efficient. Every so often, a back-up hard copy should be printed.

Very few researchers bother to photocopy their hardback A4 address book. However, a contacts book is so vital to both researchers and producers that I have never heard of anyone losing it. TV people are more security conscious than MI6 and do not leave their lap-tops at Paddington Station!

Some contacts are so sensitive they should not be disclosed. After working a few years in the industry you'll have confidential numbers which cannot be bandied around. It is not merely a matter of security but a wider issue of privacy. Personnel departments won't reveal home phone numbers and nor should researchers. If you are scared of your electronic system being insecure, even with a password, then use a paper-based system – but don't lose the book.

Whichever system you use, record all names and addresses in the contacts book even if you don't use them or consider them particularly useful for the future. You may not phone them today but it's surprising how often you want them later. The paper system is easier to keep up to date as it merely involves jotting down names whilst holding the phone in the other hand. Home phone numbers, mobile numbers, work numbers, e-mail addresses are all stored. It can be helpful to note addresses as well, but as speed of contact is crucial, phone numbers are usually more useful.

- Every time you get a lead, write in the name and number.

- Don't forget to include what the people do – e.g. clog dancer, stamp designer, astronomer, expert on molecular chemistry.

A double entry system is invaluable; list the clog dancer under *clog* as well as under the surname. When filming in Lowestoft, enter useful names under L for Lowestoft and T for Tourist Information, P for Police and so on. This sounds simplistic and doubles the work but finding someone or something quickly is essential. Names are quickly forgotten under tight deadlines and fast-changing projects.

Job advertisements often stipulate a 'good contacts book'. Not only does the contacts book follow your career, making life easier as researcher and producer, but it also gets you a job. There is an apocryphal tale from *L!ve TV* of how, after the Canary Wharf bomb explosion outside the television headquarters, Kelvin MacKenzie demanded his researchers phone up commentators and politicians at home but, as his researchers were mainly students and not journalists, no-one had a contacts book listing politicians or other worthies. Even though they were in the midst of the bomb, they missed the scoops.

On *Today*, Radio 4's flagship and other news and current affairs programmes, the researchers and journalists keep politicians' and cabinet ministers' home phone numbers together with experts such as academics, businessmen and government press officers.

LE researchers and producers list celebrities' home phone numbers and those of agents, record companies A & R (artists and repertoire) representatives. Eccentrics and experts are also useful. Generalists will collect an eclectic mix because they never know what programme they will work on next.

And where are these numbers found?

- Time and experience.

- Producers and researchers who have worked on similar shows (hence the perpetuation of the *Vanessa* scandal).

- Agents and managers (who rarely give them out for the same reason as personnel departments).

- Contributors themselves. After all, you may need to phone them to explain change of plans and so forth.

Many people, especially celebrities, are cagey about revealing their personal numbers. The reason is obvious; to protect their privacy. Some unscrupulous journalists hound them for stories. Above all, they don't want to be phoned in the middle of the night and, sadly, there *are* dangerous people out there. Who needs reminding of Jill Dando's murder?

## GENERAL TELEPHONE CONTACT NUMBERS

The Phone Book is always the first stop. Nowadays, this is organised into two sections, business numbers at the front and residential at the back. Because of cost considerations, most firms are only issued with the local phone directory but switchboards often hold the entire collection.

Don't underestimate the benefit of Directory Enquiries – 192 – which charges for its service. Some companies are understandably wary of an unlimited use of the 192 service as it escalates their phone bills. Directory Enquiries permits two searches on one call. British Telecom now runs an Internet directory service on www.bt.com/phonenet.uk, which, if your system is automatically connected to the Internet, is cheaper (or 'free' depending on your system) than phoning 192. However, a person is usually more efficient and helpful than a machine.

Mobile phone systems also have directory enquiries but, again, these are chargeable and, in my experience, are comparatively inefficient. They will, however, text the phone number into your mobile system.

Directory enquiry operators, including the BT Internet service and 192.com, require a town as they cannot do a global search. Not only is it too time consuming but it also throws up hundreds of similar names. If you haven't a clue where the person or company you are seeking is based, this is a major flaw in the system. However, there are ways round it.

BT's rival on the Internet is 192.com and several large companies, including the BBC, subscribe to it because (at the time of writing) it offers a cheaper service than phoning 192 charging 2p per enquiry after the initial (free) first twenty searches per month. Because 192.com cross-references to the electoral register (see later in the chapter) this service may throw up all relevant (and similar) names in your search. Without the town, however, there isn't enough information for a directory enquiries search. A potential snag is that this system works on *official* names, in other words what is listed in the electoral register. Not everyone is known by their first name and nicknames are, obviously, not listed. BBC employees can access 192.com via the Intranet system.

No directory enquiry service will give out ex-directory numbers and it can be difficult to find cable company numbers from rival phone companies.

## Yellow Pages and local business directories

For finding business and company phone numbers, try Yellow Pages. Talking Yellow Pages is a free phone service and is also on the Internet.

The first few pages of Yellow Pages and business directories such as Thomsons hold a mine of information and are often overlooked. True, the information found here can be found elsewhere but this information is virtually instant and free; no phone calls to pay and copies are provided free of charge or at very low cost. These directories are invaluable for local business numbers rather than London head offices.

Depending on which directory is used, there are local maps and street plans and local phone numbers for the following:

• local government offices;

• parliamentary local constituency offices;

• helplines as wide ranging as phobic societies through to old age welfare and victim support;

• travel and public transport contacts;

• road and weather watch;

• places of interest;

• sport and leisure;

• entertainment venues;

• auction houses;

• street markets.

## Electoral registers

All citizens of the UK over 18 are legally obliged to register themselves on the electoral register in order to vote in elections. The maximum fine for not doing so is currently £1,000 although prosecutions are rare. The electoral registers are public documents compiled by local authorities and available for perusal in local libraries and post offices. The electoral registers are organised in constituencies on a street-by-street, house-by-house basis. They are paper-based and published locally so there is no centralised database. Anyone visiting their local library or post office to view it cannot make photocopies or take it away with the result that a search for someone living in Exeter is difficult for anyone based in Leeds. It is time consuming and frustrating running one's eye over a list of streets in the hope of spotting the relevant name and the chances are high that, even if the name is there, it is missed.

The electronic age is changing all this, although with legislation change in the pipeline it may still be necessary to hunt manually through an electoral register held in the local library.

Together with two other companies, ICD Publishing Ltd has a licence to key in all the electoral registers for the whole country on their 192.com service and this is cross-referenced with phone numbers. There is a name search facility which means that, theoretically, one can type in a name and magically everyone with that name pops up on screen. There is an ethical problem with privacy and mistaken identity and 192.com has a policy of 'I see you, you see me' whereby anyone who is searched for has an e-mail sent to them revealing the seeker's identity.

As with everything, there are several drawbacks. The Representation of the People's Act 2000 has made a provision for people who want anonymity to opt out of their name being published on the electoral register. At the moment, the electoral register is sold commercially and this Act will prevent that – just as going ex-directory on the telephone system prevents commercial companies using phone numbers. In the future, it is likely that two copies of the electoral register will be issued; the first containing *all* names and available only to election offices, MPs and for specific stipulated purposes. This will be the one available in post offices and libraries. The second copy, only containing the names of those who have not opted out, will be sold to commercial companies at cost price. This is the version that 192.com and the other licensed companies will have although at the time of writing, the opt out provision had not come into force and no date set for its introduction.

The second drawback is that, regardless of whether it is published on CD Rom, the World Wide Web or on paper, it is out of date as soon as someone moves house. From February 2001, those eligible to vote can register as and when they move and the register will be updated on the first of each month. The annual canvas of Electoral Register forms will, as now, be sent out annually to all UK residential premises during September and October with the official date of residence being 15th of October and the official register publication date being 1st December.

Again, it must be noted that ex-directory and some cable company phone numbers will not be cross-referenced with the electoral register system on the 192.com service.

## OTHER RESEARCH SOURCES

### Clippings service

In-house libraries of large media companies often run a clippings (sometimes called cuttings) service. Each day the staff search the day's newspapers, cutting out articles on current issues, celebrities and businessmen, stamp them with the date and name of the source newspaper and file them in folders. Any company employee can theoretically borrow the files although there may be an in-house charge for the service. These files are an invaluable source of background information.

### Press Association

The most famous commercial clipping and news library is run by the Press Association in London, the national news agency of the UK and the Republic of Ireland. It operates 24 hours a day, every day of the year, supplying editorial copy for news and sport, photographs, weather and listings to the broadcast, electronic media and print industries transmitting an average of 1,500 stories and 1,000 pictures a day.

Their news library is an invaluable archive resource consisting of 14 million cuttings in the news library and more than 5 million pictures in the news photo library.

Anybody can use the PA library which is open Monday to Friday from 8 a.m. until 8 p.m. with shorter hours at the weekend. The sliding charge is currently £38 (plus VAT) for the first hour. There is a reduction for students. Although it is reviewed annually, this charge has remained the same for several years. For those unable to travel to London, there is a research service currently costing £50 (plus VAT) per hour. Many companies have a subscription to the service but everyone else must pay on site.

Other cuttings agencies are listed in *The Guardian Media Guide*.

Information from cuttings is secondary research and occasionally inaccurate. At a basic level, names are incorrectly spelt and the age wrong. Many a presenter has had egg on their face when confronting a guest with 'facts' that were palpably not true. 'Folklore' is perpetuated through press clippings and should always be double-checked for accuracy. The following chapter offers tips on this.

### Newspapers

Should your research require more than that found in cuttings libraries and you wish to see the newspapers themselves, copies of old newspapers are archived in libraries. Rather than allow members of the public unlimited access to what is a valuable and irreplaceable resource, libraries nowadays copy their newspapers onto either microfiche or film to be read on special machines. As old newspapers are very popular, many libraries run an advanced booking system for the readers although some operate on a drop-in basis.

Newspaper offices occasionally keep back-issues stretching to the first edition but whether or not you will be allowed to see and handle them depends on your status and that of the production company for whom you work.

Local newspapers are mainly found locally (no-one expects copies of Northampton's *Chronicle and Echo* in Carlisle) but copies of archive editions (on microfilm or microfiche) of national papers, *The Times*, the *Daily Telegraph*, the *Guardian*, etc., are held in central main libraries. Many of these libraries also have microfilm or microfiche photocopying facilities. (There are copyright issues in photocopying from newspapers although it is permissible for *individual* research.) The British Library (see later in the chapter, p. 28) also houses newspapers in Colindale, London.

## Books

Apart from directories, books are not generally the first port of call for a media researcher; there often isn't time before transmission to read them. However, documentaries and heavyweight programmes with a longer pre-production schedule may need substantial background information.

Libraries are under considerable budgetary restraint nowadays and up-to-date specialist reference books are, on the whole, more likely to be located in larger branches of high street bookshops. You are best advised spending a few hours browsing in a bookshop and spending the programme budget there.

## In-house libraries

Production offices usually cannot afford their own copies of the more expensive directories, especially those only used occasionally, but some large television companies have in-house libraries where directories, encyclopaedias and dictionaries are kept for general reference.

For companies too small to have their own, the commercial and reference sections at the local library is a helpful resource. A phone call is often all that is required, but a local library is for the community, not for the everyday use of lazy researchers.

Books and directories held in the reference sections of local libraries usually cannot be loaned out.

## Inter-library loan system

Older books and standard reference texts will be found in libraries and it may be worth, if the time scale permits, going through the inter-library loan system. Larger media institutions with in-house library facilities can do this for you although it may take four weeks or more for a book to arrive and the loan may run out before the production schedule. Books can be renewed if someone else has not reserved it. Fines are incurred for books returned late.

## Archives

For seriously profound and specialised research, archaeological or historical documentaries, etc., you may wish to delve into archives. Start with the local university, the Public Record Office at Kew or, as a last resort the British Library in St Pancras, London.

## The British Library

The British Library is a last resort and really only of use to specialist researchers working on, for instance, an in-depth documentary. As it is in St Pancras, London, it is expensive for companies based in the provinces who must pay overnight expenses.

There is no browsing of books at the British Library; this is a research library and not for public reference – the material held is far too precious and, in many cases, fragile. Anyone wishing to research here must prove that no other library can supply the required information. Of course, there may well be occasions when the British Library holds the items you want to film and information about obtaining filming permission is found in Chapter 8.

For those finding themselves at the last resort stage (and unless the researcher is working on an in-depth documentary, they are unlikely to need the British Library) the British Library is an unsurpassed, world-renowned depository for 16 million books and periodical volumes, 660,000 newspaper titles, 295,000 manuscripts, 260,000 India Office records, 8 million philatelic items, 4 million maps, 1.4 million music scores, 1.1 million sound discs, 184,000 sound tapes and 205,000 photographs either housed there or in Yorkshire.

In order to access its material, it is necessary to have a reader's ticket organised through the Reader Admissions Office. Certain criteria must be met and all applicants are interviewed. If the admission criteria is met, the applicant need only fill in a registration card and provide proof of identity bearing a signature (cheque card, driving licence, passport).

For security and preservation reasons most of the Library's collection is housed in closed access storage and must be ordered up for viewing, which takes approximately one hour if the material is stored in the building. The vast majority of the collection is stored in St Pancras but, for material housed elsewhere, expect to wait up to one working day before the material is available. Pencils only are allowed in the Rare Books and Manuscripts reading rooms and rare and fragile material is viewed at desks in close proximity to a staffed enquiry point.

## The Internet

To use a television term, the Internet is sexy. It is also increasingly useful and media workers who remember the primeval days pre-Internet cannot believe how they managed without it. In fact, writing this book would have been far harder and difficult to achieve without the World Wide Web.

However useful as a research tool it is, it is not a be all and end all and there are several pitfalls. The most common assumption is believing that, because of its very nature, all Internet information is copyright free and accurate. Nothing is further from the truth.

Anyone can have a Web page on the Internet and it is filled with whatever the author fancies, and the content may well be their own opinion and not based on fact at all. Also, unless the authors took the photos themselves, drew or owns the rights to the pictures or the music, they may not have permission to use them.

The copyright issues of pictures, photos and music are of no importance if you are merely seeking information, but the *accuracy* of that information is. A company will not publish how awful an employer they are, how they cheat their customers or are losing money hand over fist – although when reading their company accounts, this may become apparent.

Official sites are likely to be reliable but even these have their own agendas, their own spin on events and what they want you to be aware of. Web pages only publish what they want you to read. These sites do, however, offer contact addresses and phone numbers and may link you to other sources. It is also more likely that official sites have permission to publish copyright material but, just because they do, it doesn't mean you can too.

As for accuracy, official sites are also more likely to get information right.

No-one knows how many pages there are on the Internet, although estimates run to billions. It is tempting to browse through all the search engines printing off, at random, huge numbers of pages which *may* be relevant. A friend of mine asked a researcher to find the source of a specific quote from the actress

Candice Bergen. She faxed batches of thirty pages of useless information at a time, tying up his phone line for half-an-hour and gobbling extremely expensive fax paper because the information 'might be useful'. She never found the quote but faxed *everything* on Candice Bergen, nothing highlighted and obviously nothing read.

The point of this anecdote? When asked for specific information, find that and nothing else. Extraneous information is irrelevant and extremely irritating. Act as editor; don't expect the presenter, writer or producer to waste their precious time doing your job. In the end, it's your job that goes.

## AN EXAMPLE OF RESEARCH METHODS

A researcher is often required to find statistics along the lines of 'What is the percentage of left handers in the UK?' or 'How many women have eating disorders?'

Questions like this are, to be frank, often badly phrased and as soon as you start researching you realise that there is no simple answer. You'll ask a question and get another in return. Male or female? Over what age? Living in which part of the country? And so on.

Assuming you have never done anything like this before, where do you start? The following are suggestions; there are plenty of other routes.

First, how about an official government department? The Office of Population, Census and Surveys Office (the OPCS, commonly known as the Census Office) cannot help. The OPCS covers demographic data, which, because the census takes place every ten years, means their information and statistics may be up to ten years out of date. You might try the Department of Health.

Another starting place could be academia, university statistics departments or medical institutions, for instance. The trick is to find the expert. Start with the local university and work out.

Is there an association covering your topic? An Eating Disorder Society? Check in a directory of associations. Societies often compile research statistics and are always a useful source of information.

Remember, you may need to corroborate your figures and prove their accuracy, therefore jot down the names and phone numbers of everyone you speak to. It is also vital to make notes. No-one can remember everything.

Each time you make a phone call, put the contact person's name in your contacts book and ask them for suggestions of where to go next. Sheer detective work. The more research of this nature you do, the easier it becomes as you pick up tips and shortcuts and file them in the contacts book.

## THE DEPARTMENT OF STATE, GOVERNMENT AGENCIES/QUANGOS

Finding phone numbers and contacts for these is, as is everything, simple when you know how. The trick is to know which agency is responsible for what. The Departments of State are:

- Prime Minister's Office;

- Agriculture, Fisheries and Food;

- Cabinet Office;

- Culture, Media and Sport;

- Ministry of Defence;

- Education and Employment;

- Environment, Transport and Regions;

- Foreign and Commonwealth;

- Health;

- Home Office;

- International Development;

- Law Officers' Department;

- Lord Advocate's Department;

- Lord Chancellor's Department;

- Northern Ireland Office;

- Privy Council Office;

- Scotland Office;

- Social Security;

- Trade and Industry;

- Treasury;

- Welsh Office.

The springboard for locating any government office or quango is the government website at www.open.gov.uk.

QUANGO is an acronym for QUasi Autonomous Non-Governmental Organisation; in other words, public service bodies run as private businesses. Examples of these include: British Coal, the British Council, the Broadcasting Complaints Commission, the Civil Aviation Authority, the Commission for Racial Equality, English Heritage, the Railway Inspectorate. There are dozens of them.

## USEFUL DIRECTORIES

Apart from the obvious sources such as phone books, several specialist directories are published annually. Useful directories to be aware of are listed in the Appendix, and a few are mentioned several times in this book. Some are indispensable, whereas others may merely be referred to occasionally.

The most useful is *The Media Guide*.

It lists phone numbers (no addresses) for (amongst others):

* the departments of state;
* quangos;
* local government bodies;
* the legal system;
* prisons;
* embassies;
* the military, police and fire brigade HQs;
* trade unions;
* large company HQs;
* transport;
* education;
* national sports bodies;
* pressure and advice groups;
* together with lists of newspapers, magazines, television and radio companies, news organisations, etc.

There is also a guide to the previous year's major media events.

This is a must-have book but be warned, because of its very nature, the phone numbers and addresses may be out of date on publication. A useful tip is to write down names next to their entry in the book and because the book is so wide-ranging and difficult to negotiate at times, list regularly-used contacts in your own contacts book.

## COPYRIGHT ISSUES

There has been a lot of media coverage about Napster publishing music to download on the Web. Copyright and piracy issues are dealt with later but music, pictures and other creative works are protected by copyright whatever their source and *must* have their status checked prior to transmission.

## ACCURACY

- The information found in books and newspapers is only as accurate as the work that went into it. Far be it from me to raise suspicion about secondary research, but please be aware that not everything is accurate. How many times have you read a newspaper where the name is wrong?

- People have their own prejudices, bias and agendas and often interpret material in their own way.

- The more eminent the source, the more likely the information is correct but, whenever possible and time permitting, double-check your facts.

The Broadcasting Standards Commission, ITC and Radio Authority all refer specifically to the importance of accuracy. If there is a problem, it is better to find out before transmission or the implications can be enormous. At the very least, you will be the one writing the apology letters; at the worst, your company will have sanctions taken against it and you will be looking for another job.

## FURTHER READING

Chater, Kathy, *Production Research, An Introduction*, Focal Press, 1998.
McGuire, Mary, Stilborne, Linda, McAdams, Melinda, and Hyatt, Laurel, *Internet Handbook for Writers, Researchers and Journalists*, Guilford Press, 2000.

# 4

# People

I once answered an internal phone call at nine in the morning that started with, 'Adèle, have you ever been in a car crash?' and ended, 'Are you free for half an hour? We're on air in ten minutes and there aren't enough people in the audience. We're desperate – come and be a bum on a seat.' Can this happen today? I bet it does.

Finding people for programmes is a major role of the television and radio researcher: news and current affairs need interviewees and experts, chat shows require celebrity guests and quiz shows need contestants. The current fashion for documentary series and docu-soaps ensures programmes are virtually 'cast' beforehand. Lifestyle programmes want people with gardens or houses to makeover – even *people* for a makeover.

The researcher's brief is simple: find someone willing to take part who won't freeze on camera, has something valid to say and a personality to match.

The audience doesn't even need to like them. Casting someone in the role of villain, someone for the viewer to love to hate is as televisually important as star making. Star making, so much a consideration nowadays, is covered later in the chapter.

Locating contributors can't be done from books. However, experts write books and research papers and this is one source which, although not an immediate solution, may lead you to someone who could be useful. Once you have winkled out a name, speak to them personally. The best practice is to vet potential contributors in person – production schedule permitting.

However, some programme schedules are so tight that it is impossible to meet every contributor. Daytime chat shows such as *Vanessa*, *The Time*, *The Place* and the American imports, *Ricki Lake*, *Oprah* and *Jerry Springer* are examples of such tight pre-production scheduling that it is common for production researchers to book *everyone* over the phone. For *Jerry Springer*, the researchers follow a checklist along the lines of 'How much do you weigh? Do you have any tattoos or other disfigurements?' The viewer gets the impression that the more outlandish the contributors, the better, and certainly the ratings endorse this.

## HONESTY CLAUSES

The BBC now insists on all contributors signing honesty clauses, a policy whereby programme contributors confirm their status and identity. There is still no guarantee that the contributors are genuine, the most determined impostor is hard to detect, but the policy goes some way to getting the researchers – and the programme – off the hook and confirming programme credibility.

The policy is not infallible. In 1999 a reporter from the *Sun* answered a newspaper advertisement and masqueraded as a barmaid 'addicted to love and sex' for a programme in the BBC *Everyman* series. Although an honesty clause had been signed, the programme makers independently went through a number of checks to verify her story. These included: checking her mail at her flat during filming to ensure it corresponded, checking her name with *Spotlight* (the actors' directory) to ensure she wasn't an actress, talking to 'friends' to authenticate her story and asking if they could film at the pub where she worked. This she turned down in 'order to protect her job' (BBC News Release dated 29 June 1999). Unfortunately, even after such stringent checks the programme was dropped prior to transmission because they discovered the 'barmaid' was a fraud.

Honesty clauses are now routine but you are still advised to triple-check everything to safeguard both programme and job.

## CHAT SHOWS

Generally, two types of people appear on chat shows: members of the general public with a story embellishing the theme of the day, and the celebrity guest.

### General public contributor

Cue Andy Warhol's chance for fame; the chat show with an audience of millions and the chance to spill the beans about meeting a burglar face-to-face. The car accident that saved a life. The boyfriend who slept with mother and brother. The deeply personal to the deeply boring. The sublime to the ridiculous. And you, the researcher, must find the people with the stories. And the show is tomorrow. Or this morning.

There are several established, reliable and reputable methods to find guests. A researcher will use a combination of them.

A common one is for the end of a show request. Usually this takes the form of an onscreen slide of the programme logo and a voiceover (often the presenter) requesting people with opinions and experience of the next topic to phone in. A contact number is given together with details of when to call. Depending on the time of transmission, programme researchers are available to take calls or there is an answering machine and researchers call back the following day.

Another method is the newspaper advert. For this to be effective there must be ample pre-production time making this an established method for documentaries rather than chat shows. Depending on the programme budget, an ad is placed in several newspapers aimed at potential contributors. The downside is that many people take too long to summon up the courage to reply whilst others hoard newspapers so long that responses appear some months after the ad originally appeared.

By negotiating with listing magazines like the *TV Times* or with local journalists, it is possible to 'advertise' free (and gain pre-transmission publicity) by turning the request into a small newspaper feature: the 'fancy yourself on TV' approach.

Whichever method is chosen, a contact name and number, together with a short description of the type of person or story required, must be included in the text. It is unwise to use personal phone numbers and good policy to connect the phone to an answerphone for out-of-hours calls. This both filters out crank calls and aids potential contributors who cannot use the phone during the day. If possible, give a date by when to call.

Expect a large number of time-wasters and cranks.

Trawling magazine and newspaper articles often throws up suitable people but is a matter of luck and spotting the article at the right time. (It is a good idea to file away unusual hobbies or stories and refer to the file at frequent intervals.) Contacting people from articles involves phoning the relevant newspaper or magazine and asking for the journalist who wrote the original article or the picture desk editor (if a photograph has been printed) for the contact name and phone number. Although some newspapers are cagey about revealing names and addresses, most are happy to pass on the information to fellow professionals (so much for privacy and confidentiality). Occasionally payment for the contact number is requested. This tends to be from freelance journalists or a local news agency scrabbling to make a living. Whether or not the payment is made depends on the programme budget and how desperate the producer is for the contributor.

If a newspaper article inspired a programme topic in the first place, inclusion of the featured person is an added bonus.

Using contacts from personnel working on other programmes. Swapping names and addresses between production teams is a well-trodden method and is where the *Vanessa* team came unstuck. Relying on a source of over-exposed controversial contributors is bad practice and to be avoided at all costs.

However, swapping contacts is an established way of locating suitable programme guests and can be legitimate if used *judiciously* and scrupulously. By chatting to fellow professionals who have used the contributors before, you can confirm how well the guest performs and their value to the programme.

I have seen the same professional virgin a few times over the past fifteen years on programmes made by different TV stations. She is intelligent, articulate and, as far as I or anyone else knows, still holding out for the perfect man. Her name is in my contact book. When she finds Mr Right, the next theme is – women who waited!

## Selection processes for chat shows

Not everyone is suitable to appear on television. Put another way, some people are better than others. Who to choose depends on how good the other potential contributors' stories are, how well the person talks and how you actually feel about them. A lot of it is gut feeling. The more sensational and provocative the story, the better the television but, for balance and mix, include the mundane as well. Also, the more sensational and outrageous, the more chance the story is invented.

Depending on the subject to be covered, the questions to ask potential contributors are:

- name;
- age;
- their story;
- town where they live/come from;
- phone number and address;
- are they free and willing to come along to the recording?

Programmes aim for a balance of age and gender but this is prescribed by the subject matter itself; a programme on prostate cancer is unlikely to feature women unless they are older and accompanying their husbands.

Onscreen arguments make good television. A contributor may be chosen simply to offer an extreme and opposing view, however frivolous, prejudiced and specious their point. Beware. The BBC, BSC, ITC and Radio Authority regulate taste, decency and offence to public feeling, published in their Pro-gramme Codes. It is also important to ensure that contributors

> are not coached or pushed or improperly induced into saying anything which they know not to be true or do not believe to be true.
>
> Broadcasting Standards Commission, Fairness paragraph 4 (vi)

The residence of the contributor is an issue depending on the location of the recording studios and whether the programme is made for local or national transmission. A local programme has contributors from around the region; the viewer doesn't want someone from Billericay if the programme is centred in Bradford. However, for a networked programme, the viewer in Carlisle is excluded if everyone on TV is from Croydon.

A consideration to bear in mind is how the contributor gets to the recording studio. It is great television to have someone from a northerly Scottish Isle and a thick regional accent, but the amount of time they spend on the train, and whether they arrive on time for the recording, must be considered. Chat shows are cheap, cheerful and made on a shoestring budget. Some pro-grammes pay travel expenses, some don't. The cost of transporting someone from one end of the country to the other is a drain on the budget, especially if hotels and planes are included.

Payment? This is a difficult question. Most people are only too willing to appear free for those fifteen minutes of fame. However, anyone paid by the hour loses money if they take time off work and these, alongside those who assume television companies are oozing with money, expect to be paid. As some programmes include out-of-pocket and travel expenses in the budgets and some don't, confirm any payment beforehand with the producer before mentioning it over the phone. On the other hand, if it hasn't been raised beforehand, it is embarrassing when a researcher must explain in studio that there is no payment. However, in my experience, those wanting or expecting a fee mention it beforehand.

Experts should be and expect to be paid. Some stations, notably the BBC, have set (notoriously low) fees, the rate depending on the contributor's status. Other companies negotiate. Negotiable fees are generally between £30 and £100 (the lower the better) and depend on the type of show, the budget, the expert's contribution, the length of time they are required and how desperate the producer is to include them.

Finally, never confirm anyone over the phone without checking with the pro-ducer first unless you are absolutely sure about who else is on or are in sole charge of who appears. This way, the balance of the programme is ensured and will not be one-sided. Unless you are totally certain, always leave the option of backing out by promising to phone them back.

## CELEBRITY GUESTS FOR CHAT SHOWS, GAME SHOWS, DAYTIME PROGRAMMES

The casting department is the established route for booking actors and actresses for television and radio drama, and they are responsible for drawing up contracts and negotiating Equity rates. Researchers are never involved. However, in large companies, the casting department is too busy to find guests for LE and children's programmes and this job becomes the responsibility of the programme researcher who has the added advantage of knowing exactly what the programme requires in terms of personality, style and content.

Depending on one's view, this job may be regarded as the best or worst in television. For those who regard it as the *best* in television, the job of celebrity booker is paradise and in some cases one person has the sole responsibility of booking them. It is perhaps more usual for several researchers on a show to suggest and book celebrity guests.

An up-to-date knowledge of celebrity tittle-tattle and gossip is crucial.

- Now is the time to subscribe to *Hello!*, *OK!*, *Chat* and other gossip magazines.

- Get on the mailing list for publishers, theatres and record companies.

- Keep up with musical trends from what's on at *The Proms*, which groups are in the Top 10 and who's touring and where.

- Watch the television soaps.

- Go to the cinema and theatre.

- Subscribe to *The Stage*, *Music Week* and any other specialist industry journals.

- Read the sports pages, fashion pages and the *What's On* guide in your local paper.

Who is in, who is out and who is up and coming?

Match the guest to the audience of your show and to the budget. Guests themselves are self-limiting. You might be under the impression that huge Hollywood stars and pop groups won't get out of bed for an audience of less than several million but persuading an agent or manager that your show is *influential* might convince them that it is worth their client appearing on your programme even without the huge audience to boost the book, film or public image. Some stars will appear on your show because it sounds fun, others because *Parkinson* pulls practically anyone and others because it may boost their sales or put money in their pocket. Let's face it; minor celebrities desperate to keep in the public eye will appear on anything. The question is, do you want them on *your* show? Or again, can you afford to be choosy?

Finding guests who are approved of by even the fussiest of producers (those disliking minor celebrities nobody has heard of) can be a daunting and dispiriting task. Pulling off a coup, though, gives a huge boost to your self-satisfaction, esteem and career.

*Thesps, turns, celebs, artistes* and *guests* are synonyms used. Although not rude, the first two are the least polite and it isn't recommended to use these terms in the hearing of humourless guests or agents. Those with a sense of humour don't care and use ruder expressions to describe themselves. *Thesps*, incidentally, is short for thespians (actors), and *turns* usually refer to variety acts such as jugglers, vents (ventriloquists) and singers.

It goes without saying that demand influences price. The more popular the potential guest, the more work they have (film, theatre, television series) the harder they are to book and, for drama especially, the higher the fee. For chat shows and one-off appearances in LE, the cost is often irrelevant. What is more important is whether the celebrity wants or has time to take part.

There are exceptions to this. Some guests appear on television or radio for free simply to promote their book, record, film, new TV series or theatrical tour. The trick is to get them on your programme first before everyone is sick to death of them.

Working with famous people can involve the tact of a siege negotiator. Some celebrities are brilliant onscreen but impossibly temperamental. Others are tremendous value if kept away from the prerecording booze. Some are notoriously unreliable and fail to arrive at the very last minute. Some won't talk to anyone less than a producer. Others only travel by plane even if that is the most inconvenient method to get them to studio. Some expect the backstage to be cleared before they go on and others must be the centre of attention, telling appallingly tasteless jokes in warm-up. Others are excruciatingly shy.

There again, some of the biggest stars are delightfully easy to work with and buy the entire crew presents at the end of the production.

In short, beware the following difficult celebrity guests:

- the demanding and temperamental;
- those who can't talk without a script;
- the snob, the alcoholic, the sexist and the sex maniac.

When hearing rumours, phone up a colleague and ask their opinion. It may be too late to make replacements or the guest may be so sensational in principle that the production team are prepared to take a risk, but at least you are forewarned and can prepare a strategy of how to deal with them.

## Agents and managers

Agents and personal managers represent actors and a host of celebrities from sporting stars, television presenters, variety acts, weather presenters and people like Maureen from *Driving School*. For a fee, usually 10 or 15 per cent of their income, an agent manages their client's career, negotiates fees and acts as intermediary between client and employer.

For films, theatre productions and television or radio drama, casting agents negotiate the contracts on behalf of the production company. For one-off appearances in television or radio programmes the researcher, assistant producer or producer make the booking but the casting department usually sends out the contract.

It *is* possible to go direct to the celebrity, although this is potentially problematic especially if the cold caller doesn't know the celebrity personally. Actors often prefer all work to go via their agent and many agents are upset if their clients are approached individually as it can lead to double-booking. Most celebrities inform their agents anyway to avoid conflicting dates whereas others are only too happy to keep the full fee! For best practice, all approaches should be via the agent. In an emergency, a researcher or producer with an hour to magic up a replacement guest will, of necessity, phone up a celebrity direct if they know them personally.

Agents' books change constantly. They will take on new presenters and actors and shed the less popular/economic ones. Agents occasionally poach each other's clients although this is unprofessional and understandably frowned upon.

## Finding agents and managers

How do you find who represents whom and their number?

The directory for actors and actresses is *Spotlight*. In book form, it is published in eight volumes: 20,000 actors and actresses are showcased under separate sections, e.g. lead and character actors, in each volume. The actor's photograph is published with details of height and eye colour and the name, address and phone number of their theatrical agent. Although casting departments have up-to-date versions, few production offices can afford their own copies. For those registered as subscribers, CD Roms are supplied together with an online service. At the time of writing, the subscription was £99 (plus VAT) for one user for one year or, for more than one user, £99 (plus VAT) for the first and £25 for each additional user. The cost for one user for three months was £30 (plus VAT). *Spotlight* casting on the Web includes a comprehensive search facility and CVs of over 25,000 professional actors, actresses, presenters, students, children, stunt artists, fight directors, Directors' Guild of Great Britain, walk-ons, supporting artists, choreographers and designers.

*Spotlight* also publishes a directory of presenters who generally are not represented by theatrical agents but by specialist personal managers. Peter Powell, an ex-presenter himself, is one of the better known. Personal managers are happy and willing to send out client lists and pinning these on the wall or filing them aids speedy reference. Lists must be regularly updated – presenters change their management company (or, like the Spice Girls, drop them). And personal managers, like theatrical agents, take on new clients and drop the passé.

Sports personalities, variety acts (ventriloquists, jugglers, comedians, contortionists, etc.), singers and other non-specific celebrities are not in *Spotlight*'s brief but are also represented by agents.

For footballers, cricketers and sportsmen who are still playing, the first approach is via their club. For anyone retired from the game, it is a matter of finding who represents them. A lot of these are on the after-dinner speaker circuit and *The White Book* or *Celebrity Services* are as good a place to look as anywhere but the local television, radio or newspaper sports desk often have a contact too.

For athletes still competing and younger sportsmen – Olympic hopefuls, for instance – try Sport England or the relevant governing sporting body. Again, the local sports desk may be helpful. However, if the athletes are under 16, refer to the rules governing children found later in this chapter. Another source is the sports promoters. For boxing, for instance, the first port of call is Frank Warren's office. Former sports personalities who have taken to performing in pantomimes often have a theatrical agent as well.

*Variety acts* – jugglers, vents, contortionists and other speciality acts (colloquially, *spesh* acts) are rare nowadays except in LE or talent programmes, and are very reliant on the vagaries of fashion. Speciality acts are a dying art, which is a shame, and are ripe for rediscovery. Because they are so very unfashionable, it is increasingly hard to find exponents. Scouring live venues and the comedy circuit is pretty hit-and-miss, but LE production personnel do this as a matter of course, trawling the Edinburgh Fringe Festival and others to discover acts. Finding a ventriloquist for next week is more difficult unless you personally know one. The same goes for other performers. There *are* agents who specialise in these but beware the children's entertainer syndrome; the semi-professional, little better than Great Uncle Harry, adding a few quid to his pocket by entertaining children on Saturday afternoons. Acts such as jugglers, contortionists and escapologists often make their living as street entertainers. If you spot one, get their details but such performers are nomadic by their very nature and work Europe-wide where the takings are better. In my experience, contortionists on local agents' books are little better than good gymnasts.

A major source for speciality acts is *The White Book*, a directory of specialist events and contacts in the music industry, music production and corporate event work. This is now on-line at www.whitebook.co.uk and, at the time of writing, did not require subscription or registration. There is a search facility which, if *escapologist* is typed in, throws up at least a dozen references.

There are thousands of hopefuls out there waiting for the big break. Agents exist for these unknown singers and dancers too but the quality is variable and it may be worth asking the casting department for suggestions. Stage, music colleges and drama schools are another source. Equity and the Musician's Union have lists of reputable establishments. Local stage schools will bend over backwards for publicity. The casting department, who have close contacts with all stage schools, will set up auditions but, to be honest, very few researchers are involved in finding new faces unless they are working on a talent show, in which case the production office will be *deluged* with wannabees and agents.

*Where are they now?* Television is an all-consuming monster, idolising one day, discarding the next. Once-household names disappear off the face of the earth or at least off the airwaves and can prove most elusive to trace. Agents have dropped them from their books and the casting department hasn't heard of them for years. These are the people who crop up in the bankruptcy court spotted by a keen-eyed journalist scanning the court lists. Finding one is largely a matter of luck and graft. The cuttings library may provide a lead, the former agent may have kept in touch on a friendship basis, the gossip columnists on the national papers may know. If they appear in the obituary columns, you are too late.

*Bands, singers and groups* with recording contacts are contactable via their labels. Most recording companies are London-based but some large influential ones are in the provinces. The recording companies A & R (Artists and Repertoire) department's responsibility is to look after the company's signings and they bend over backwards to get their group on your show. They accompany the band, often organise travel arrangements and keep an eye on clothing, behaviour and any other problems likely to be encountered. In other words, they are minders for the band. Some groups have managers touting the media stations for appearances and publicity and, once the group is to appear, take the same function as the A & R Department in that they organise all the travel and other arrangements. The issues involved with bands and musical acts are treated at length in Chapter 7.

*Authors* – which include actors, presenters, sports personalities, explorers and anyone famous who has written a book – are contactable through the publisher. If an actor has written a book, this effectively circumvents their agent. When a publisher promotes a book, a publisher's representative may well accompany the author to the studio with the publisher taking responsibility and paying for the travel arrangements. This is not always the case, so check beforehand. To find the publisher, the easiest way is to phone the local bookshop or library and ask them to check for you. Publishers' addresses and phone numbers are listed, amongst other directories, in *The Writers' and Artists' Yearbook*, *The Writer's Handbook* and *The Media Guide* but once the relevant publisher has been ascertained, getting the phone number is a cinch.

*Foreign celebrities* are contacted in very similar ways. Many larger agencies have a US branch and most have USA and European contacts. Start with your UK sources and contacts and work out from there.

*Celebrity Service Ltd* provides the *Celebrity Bulletin* on subscription, a twice-weekly publication (usually one or two A4 sheets) listing foreign stars visiting the UK, the reason and a contact number thus providing access to guests otherwise unavailable. Included in the cost of the subscription (£70 per month at the time of writing), *Celebrity Service* acts as an information service providing celebrity biographies and will give you the name of agents and PR companies. Depending on the programme budget, subscription to this service might be helpful for those elusive Hollywood stars and non-mainstream celebrities for whom finding an agent or contact proves difficult.

If *Celebrity Service* can't help and you really have no idea how to get in touch with someone but have seen them on television, phoning the production office should supply you with the contact name and number. It occasionally happens that a celebrity has no agent. Under these circumstances, the production office will contact them for you and ask permission to give out their number. For reasons of integrity and ethics, it is doubtful if the production office will reveal the number straight away.

*Lists of agents* can be obtained from the governing body for personal managers and theatrical agents, The Personal Managers Association or, for a general list of theatrical type agents including those for artistes, models, children, extras and walk-ons try amongst others, *The Knowledge* and *The White Book*.

## Booking celebrity guests

Once the agent has been located, it ought to be a relatively easy process to book a programme guest. Unfortunately, it isn't. Clients hire agents to find the best jobs and remuneration. Theatrical agents, especially those representing serious actors, often consider a one-off appearance on a quiz show as tawdry, cheapening the credibility of the actor involved. Some agencies employ specialists to work in different fields so that an actor might have one representative for television and another for theatre. The very largest even employ representatives for the kiss-and-tell autobiography as well. On the other hand, the smallest agencies, and those preferring the personal touch, have one agent to deal with all offers of work for a client.

Agencies have many actors on their books and it often happens that, trying to cast guests for a particular series, the same agent is contacted several times with requests for different people.

There is no mystique to booking someone. The negotiations usually follow the same procedure:

* the date the celebrity is required;
* the programme – what it is and how the celebrity will be involved;
* the fee.

If, according to the agent's records, your target is free on the date stated, the agent will phone to ask if they want to take part. Like the rest of us, celebrities have lives away from the spotlight and, just because they are free doesn't mean they will take part; hospital appointments, their son's sports day, or a trip with friends may take priority. Whereas an important film part will induce them to drop everything, appearing in a chat show doesn't have the same appeal unless they need the money.

An actor working from home is also not an automatic refusal unless they are filming abroad. Someone can be considered a potential guest because they *are* filming or performing 'just down the road'. In these circumstances, it is occasionally worth contacting the stage or film producer first instead of the agent as they must give the go-ahead anyway. Producers are pretty amenable for extra publicity. Whether or not the celebrity *can* appear depends entirely on their schedule. Once the production is up and running, theatre performers are free during the day except for matinees and can be tempted to pick up an extra fee. This depends on the person involved; some are too tired during a stage run to take on anything else, others find living in a strange city palls after a while and are only too pleased to widen professional contacts.

Be prepared for rebuffs and setbacks. Don't take it personally. Many agents decline (suspiciously quickly – did they approach their clients?) and a few are patronising while they do so. Others are only too willing to help and are approachable in the extreme. Booking celebrities is a small world and word gets round as to which agent is easy to work with and which celebrity is capricious.

After a while, experience tells you that:

- some actors won't appear at all. They are either too busy, live abroad or their agents won't let them. If you succeed in getting one of these on your show, congratulate yourself;

- some performers are on exclusive contracts and *cannot* appear however much the project might interest them.

## Negotiating fees

*Equity*, the actors' union, sets recommended minimum production fees for its members but this covers *performance*. If the celebrity is to perform during their appearance, all further negotiations should go via the casting department in order to prevent major misunderstandings. There are too many legal pitfalls which the casting department have the experience and knowledge to avoid.

The Equity agreement does not cover *personal appearances* where an Equity member is being themselves and the researcher may well negotiate the fee. This is normally with the agent although on a few occasions I have discussed it with the celebrity instead. How much is offered depends on the programme budget and the producer will set the limit. Should an impasse occur, the researcher must consult the producer because if one guest is appearing for less than expected, more money is available in the kitty. Again, the producer might regard the potential guest as such good television that they are prepared to up the stakes. In some cases, once the researcher has confirmed the availability of a potential guest the producer takes the reins and negotiates fees and other contractual issues.

The casting department draws up the contract. Long gone are the days when a guest insists on being paid cash in hand in order to avoid income tax and agent's fees. If this is suggested, a quick word to the producer is recommended.

*Travel expenses* and other incidentals are normally paid and, according to the guest's status, train travel may be first class but again, check the budget. Having said that, no-one expects a big star to travel standard class and anyone suggesting it might find the guest refusing to come. Airfares are commonly barred unless the distance is considerable or there are time constraints.

However, everything is negotiable and some well-known celebrities will happily drive as long as the second-class train fare covers their petrol.

Where a guest is *promoting a product* (a book, film, single), the fee may be waived and travel expenses funded from someone else's budget – namely the record company or publisher. Film clips, copies of the book, photographs and other sundries are often supplied with the hope that they will be screened. Because copyright is often in the hands of the promoter, royalties may be waived although in the case of promoting a new film, an onscreen credit is usually mandatory. Check first. The use of film clips is discussed in the following chapter and you must refer to the ITC and RA rules about onscreen promotions.

## Bringing guests into studio

The guest has been booked so now they must turn up for the recording with the minimum of hassle, angst and problem potential. Planning is also required to ensure everything runs smoothly once they arrive in studio.

Although the casting department sends the contract to the agent, it is worth writing a letter, e-mailing or faxing the agent yourself with the following details:

- the name of the programme, date and recording time;
- the topic to be discussed or what the guest is to do;
- travel details.

It is unusual for researchers to book the train tickets but, as they are the contact point for the agent and the celebrity guest, they often liaise. In large companies, the travel desk books the tickets and either sends out the tickets or gives them to the researcher to do so. Frankly, I recommend sending the ticket direct to the celebrity rather than the agent as there is less possibility of snags. Make sure you note down the travel details first.

The celebrity may have certain requirements which the researcher, as point of contact, should pre-empt and either deal with personally or inform the relevant person. These include:

- dietary requirements. Many celebrities are vegetarian. Some are diabetic;
- special considerations, e.g. large wrestlers require reinforced chairs;
- warn floor managers, makeup and wardrobe *in advance* of considerations such as reinforced chairs. Some actresses have sensitive skin and require a special brand of makeup which may have to be brought in specially;

- book a parking space in the car park if the guest is driving.

Depending on the programme and the treatment, the director, producer and presenter also need:

- special props such as copies of books. The agent or manager can help or point you in the right direction;

- a biography and/or background notes (see p. 63).

In order to troubleshoot potential disasters, the researcher can:

- get a direct contact number for the celebrity (although most agents won't reveal them) to confirm travel arrangements in person, thus preventing misinformation and last minute changes;

- give your mobile/home phone number to the agent for emergencies after you have left the office;

- telephone the day before to confirm and check there are no unexpected hitches like illness. This leaves time to set up a replacement;

- if a guest is staying overnight at a hotel before recording, phone to confirm their safe arrival. Depending on your relationship, it may be a friendly gesture to personally check their well being.

Should the unthinkable occur and a guest fails to turn up, the more notice there is, the better. You will get excuses, some of which are true, some not, but the result is the same; a celebrity no-show.

The PA is usually responsible for assigning dressing rooms and sending the list to Reception but get a copy before the guests arrive. The floor manager or director devises the recording schedule (the running order) and again, check it in order to reassure guests when they arrive so they know exactly what is happening.

If a guest is squeezing in a job whilst performing on stage or working on a film, the timings are crucial and it is *essential* the celebrity leaves the studio on time.

The above are recommended for *all* programme contributors, although you should seriously consider whether to mete out personal phone numbers to all and sundry.

## QUIZ AND GAME SHOW CONTESTANTS

Production companies who specialise in quiz programmes often employ contestant coordinators whose entire brief is advertising, picking contestants and coordinating travel arrangements. Everything, in fact, to make the contestant search efficient. Elsewhere, researchers take on this role.

Quiz shows have specific contestant requirements. *Family Fortunes,* and *Jim Davidson's Generation Game* require relatives. For general knowledge quizzes, the brief will be a range of ages, gender, class and occupation. In *Blind Date*, the contestant is (presumably) single, attractive and personable. Some shows prefer the eccentric, others the strictly conventional.

For a not yet entirely explained sociological reason, women and ethnic minorities are under-represented on quiz shows. It isn't because they aren't picked, it's because fewer apply in the first place. In *Who Wants to be a Millionaire?* critics and viewers commented alike that few contestants were women and even fewer black. It remains one of the major challenges for the researcher to find good, competitive female and black contestants. The disabled and elderly are also under-represented.

The initial search involves advertising and one of the most common and effective methods is to make an announcement at the end of a programme during the current series. For new programmes this is not an option and adverts are placed where they are most likely to attract potential contestants. For activity-type game shows, sports centres and specialist magazines are the most obvious but regional newspapers are useful. Listings magazines, the *TV Times* for instance, can attract attention. Include a date by which the applicant must respond.

Respondents are sent application forms. The questions depend on the type of show but always include the obvious – name, address, phone number, date of birth and gender and perhaps occupation and marital status. Some request a recent photograph. For programmes involving strenuous activity, questions about fitness and health are included and for quizzes, general knowledge questions may be added. Talent shows like *Stars in their Eyes* request cassettes.

Thousands of people apply to take part in a popular programme or one with high value prizes, and the sackloads of mail can be overwhelming. Hence the question requiring an anecdotal response; this acts as an initial shortlist.

Because so many people are desperate to get onto television, potential contestants may misrepresent themselves. The *contestant tour* whittles these out. For daytime and cable programmes with limited budgets the final selection may take place over the phone.

## The contestant tour

Contestant tours are expensive. Even for one researcher working in a hotel conference room and armed with a Polaroid camera, there are the travel and hotel costs. For more elaborate programmes, *Stars in their Eyes* for instance, there may be a full production number with producer, researcher, director and perhaps musical director and video camera as well.

A common method of cost cutting is for contestants to travel to the production office and be interviewed there. This is fine for regional programmes where no-one has far to travel but is unacceptable for a networked programme where contestants come from all corners of the country.

The venue is generally in a city or large town in each of the major regions. Hotels are a popular choice because they are well known to the general public and supply maps of their location. They also supply coffee and sweets (at a charge) which is of considerable benefit when the selection process involves being cooped up between the same four walls today and all day tomorrow. A conference room at the local television or radio station will do just as well but there will be a charge.

At this initial stage, potential contestants are not reimbursed for travel costs or for taking time off work.

The tour involves considerable travelling between venues and there are several schools of thought as to the best method to tackle it. Do you:

a   travel to the next location after finishing the last audition? i.e. travel when tired but enjoying a relatively late start the following morning; or

b   travel the following morning and risk traffic jams, getting lost and setting up in a hurry?

On the whole, researchers organise their own contestant tour schedules and there are strategies for reducing stress:

• whenever possible, if going long distances, take the train and consider flying (if the budget runs to this) and car hire;

• ensure the schedule isn't ridiculously tight.

The company travel desk or production manager, if one is assigned to the programme, can order train tickets. Few production companies sanction first-class train travel.

Potential contestants are given a date, a time and venue and up to thirty or more might be seen in one morning depending on what they are expected to do. For general knowledge quizzes, this is a chance to ensure the candidates didn't cheat on the original application form and whittle out the obviously unfit for an activity or adventure-based show. The selection process depends on what contestants are expected to do on the show and the tasks range from an informal chat and those amusing anecdotes, a general knowledge or IQ test through to a full-scale audition.

There are a few guidelines on how to behave:

- a researcher is representing the company and must be polite and professional at all times;

- under no circumstances can the researcher snigger at anyone;

- nor can they turn up in Bermuda shorts and Hawaiian shirt. That researcher lost his job.

For the production team, contestant tours are exhausting: considerable travel, a succession of late nights, a different impersonal hotel each day and mass catering. It can be very dispiriting. They meet a lot of ordinary people together with the tone-deaf 'singer' for an amateur talent show, the complete ignoramus for a general knowledge quiz, faces merge into each other, the 'stars' stand out but it is difficult to remember the rest.

## Selecting the contestants

Back in base with Polaroid-enhanced memories, the choice of contestant comes down to (and not necessarily in this order):

- how they performed during the selection process;

- personality;

- gender – in some programmes, women are virtually guaranteed a place;

- ethnicity – in some programmes, non-whites are virtually guaranteed a place;

- place of residence – a balance of north, south, rural and big city;

- looks, age and occupation;

- gut feeling.

A shortlist is compiled and then each programme is 'cast', although the producer may now make the final decisions. It is important to screen out anyone who has been convicted of serious offences and, as in documentaries and chat shows, it is common policy for contestants to sign a declaration in which they agree to conform to the terms of appearance. (The BBC insists on this in its *Quiz and Game Show Producer Guidelines*.)

There are usually more short-listed potential contestants than places in the programme and the final choice rests on a number of arbitrary factors. As each series strives for a mix of people to complement each other, the aim may be to have a woman in each show and if most interviewees are men, women are picked even when comparatively weak on the personality or talent stake. The production team may want a variety of accents, working class and professional and again, this can influence the final choice. Those with a good personality who chatted easily in the contestant tour are likely to make the short-list. Those with silly stories or interesting hobbies can provide script points for the presenter. A high score for the tasks in the selection process may be an issue.

On high-profile programmes with large budgets, the entire short-list may be recalled for a second audition. During these call-back sessions, the researcher often ends up in the host or hostess role relaxing potential contestants, handing out coffee, confirming their transport home and paying expenses if these are now covered by the budget. For those who fail to make it onto the actual programme, this should go towards compensating them for their disappointment.

Occasionally contestants are held in reserve for illness and other possibilities. The reserves live relatively locally to the studios and it is essential they fully understand that they may not make it into the programme.

*Who Wants to be a Millionaire?* revolutionised the contestant search. Contestants phone a special number, answer a simple question and are picked at random by computer. The cost of the calls funds the prize money.

Once the contestants are selected, they are given a recording date or dates and their travel to the studio is arranged. Nowadays several episodes of a quiz programme are recorded in one day and there are occasions when contestants are warned that they may have an extra overnight stay. When contestants appear in the following programme if they win, all contestants must be prepared for that eventuality and bring an extra set of clothing.

Contestants are not media professionals and it is probably their first time on television. *The BBC Producers' Guidelines* (Chapter 22, 'Game Shows and Competitions', 3 Treating Contestants Fairly) states unequivocally that they must be treated honestly and fairly and gives other guidance as to their treatment.

Travel tips and advice on organising contestants can be found in the 'celebrity guest' section above.

## Clothing for contestants

Researchers are always asked what should be worn in studio. Unless there is a house style (colour coordination for instance) the answer is simple – whatever they feel comfortable in. There is one caveat, clothing with large logos and trademarks is regarded as sponsorship and not permitted. They will be asked to change it.

Some clothes are more televisual than others. Solid primary colours can flare on camera and narrow stripes or small spots are apt to strobe. Even wardrobe designers are fallible, although well aware of what *should* work. For this reason, suggest contestants bring an alternative just in case.

Wardrobe assistants are usually on hand for last-minute ironing and stitching on of loose buttons.

## AUDIENCES

Tickets for television recordings are free. The length of time it takes to record a show, the constant repositioning of cameras, the restrictions to the audience sight lines and the fact that, if mistakes are made, certain takes and links may be recorded many times, means that no television company would dare charge. Also, as the audience is often an integral part of the show, it could be argued (although no-one ever does) that perhaps the audience should be paid to be there.

The BBC and some larger television companies have special departments to fill audience seats; however, for chat shows, quizzes and LE, the researcher may be called upon to find the audience. They used to organise the travel too, although these days, with tight budgets, most audiences pay their own way.

For quizzes, offering places to those who turned up for the initial selection can fill seats. For chat shows and current affairs, people who were contacted for information, even if their anecdotes were unsuitable, have a view on the issue and may find when the cameras are rolling that they have an input. Local colleges and schools, universities, gardening societies and sports groups are reliable sources of large numbers to fill audiences (impolitely referred to as 'bums on seats').

Daytime recordings create the most logistical headaches for the audience researcher. In the not-so-distant past, the local old people's home provided banks of old ladies for afternoon recordings. Nowadays this is less common because production personnel prefer the aesthetically attractive, youthful audience. No comment.

In *Who Wants to be a Millionaire?* and the final of *Stars in their Eyes* (when voting takes place by phone or Internet and is less likely to be rigged) the audience largely consists of friends, family and contestants from previous episodes. In these cases, an accurate list of where everyone is sitting is essential for the floor manager, cameramen and director.

The audience for *University Challenge* consists of student supporters organised via the university and the general contestant research. Whether or not these audiences pay for their transport to the recording studio depends on the programme policy and budget. Under certain circumstances, the production office may organise and pay for coaches but this is increasingly rare except for new programmes unfamiliar to the general public.

The tickets sent to members of the audience should explain contractual details and health and safety issues like a no-smoking policy. It is also common policy to insert a warning clause if animals are likely to appear. This covers the television company against complaints of allergies, pregnancy and phobias. Further health and safety issues are found in Chapter 6 and in the Appendix.

As always, on the day before recording, confirm by phone that the audience is still coming. If there are only a small number of seats in studio, the loss of a fifty-seat coach load will severely affect the size of the audience and the cameramen and director will find it difficult to make the studio look full. (I remember the props department filling an audience with showroom dummies; apparently no-one noticed.)

Ensure all organisers have a contact number for emergencies – a flat tyre is a major crisis in a tight recording schedule.

Because of insurance and health and safety requirements, most studios have an age limit of sixteen (*You've Been Framed* is one of the few programmes accepting children from eight, although they must be chaperoned). Another exception is on children's programmes. The regulations governing children and television are discussed later in this chapter.

Members of an audience occasionally want to bring their children. This is normally discouraged, although if a show is about teenage single mothers, it may be a practical necessity. In such cases, ask the producer if there is money in the budget for a qualified and vetted nanny – the last thing a programme wants is a tabloid scoop about abandoned babies in the green room. The other issue is one of truancy. The law requires all children of school age to attend school and permission is required from the head teacher if a child is absent for a reason other than illness. During one of Manchester's frequent truancy sweeps, a child was caught accompanying its parents to a recording at Granada Television – with no head teacher's permission.

## EXPERTS

For reasons of impartiality, local television debates and current affairs programmes such as the BBC's *Today* on Radio 4 feature differing and opposing views. The contributors holding informed opinions tend to be experts: a politician, doctor, lawyer, historian, businessman, representative of a self-help group and so on. The researcher locates them.

In a society where the establishment is still dominated by white, middle-class, middle-aged men, the challenge is to avoid a panel of just that. Tokenism should also be avoided especially if the token woman, for instance, is not particularly strong. The researcher aims for a good mix.

Finding a politician is easy. Getting them to appear is more difficult and depends on their attitude, the topic for discussion and their availability. Members of the Cabinet are the hardest to pin down because of their schedules and overwhelming preference for appearing on influential national flagships like *Today* or the news. If you are working on this type of programme then, apart from fitting in with their schedules, there should be little problem.

Otherwise, it might be easier to aim for a local politician with a lower profile. The constituency office number is in the local phone book and their agent should be amenable. Many politicians are contactable by both phone and e-mail at the House of Commons and the main switchboard or the information office at the House can offer advice. Politicians are extremely busy and you are likely first off to speak to the MP's researcher or assistant.

Members of the European Parliament are also relatively easy to 'book' although they work and travel between Strasbourg, Brussels and the UK. The downside to MEPs is that few members of the general public know their MEP unless they are prominent like Glenys Kinnock. A sign of the times is that fewer appear to care.

Depending on the programme content, it may be obligatory to balance views with a member from an opposition party.

Prominent politicians and certainly those in the Cabinet expect a list of questions beforehand, often faxed or e-mailed prior to them agreeing to participate. There are several reasons for this. Should the question involve facts and figures they need to research the figures first. Also (excuse my cynicism) for unpalatable or controversial questions, the official 'spin' is ascertained beforehand. Politicians have been known to veto certain topics. A presenter tackling a vetoed topic is courting an onscreen row, politicians storming off in a huff and future boycott from both politician and party. Good television, yes, but if a non-biased ethos is integral to the programme, this is a serious consequence and may lead to repercussions within the television or radio station.

Once a general election is declared, the appearance of members of parliament in studio is strictly regulated. Effectively, they are now *constituency candidates* and are restricted under the Representation of the People Act 1983. This comes into force from 'the date of the dissolution of Parliament or the announcement of dissolution in the case of a parliamentary election, the issue of the writ at a by election, or five weeks before polling day for local government elections' (Representation of the People Act 1983.)

The rules can be found in Appendix 3 (8i) of the ITC Programme Code – Programmes at the time of elections and also in the BBC's Producers' Guidelines. The programme editor on the news and current affairs programmes will be well aware of such restrictions and politicians do, of course, appear all the time after a general election has been called. The main point to adhere to is that the provisions of due impartiality are observed (ITC Programme Code, Appendix 3).

A problem arises if a politician is booked to appear on a programme before an election is declared. For instance, I once booked a politician who had, as a single woman, adopted a child and she agreed to talk on a chat show about it. Between agreeing to appear and the studio recording, the election was declared. We were all aware of the upcoming election but the speed of the declaration surprised even her. This appearance was permissible because she appeared as herself with no reference to standing as a prospective member of parliament.

The actual wording in the ITC Programme Code covering her appearance is

**Non-political programmes**
Appearances by candidates as actors, musicians, singers or other entertainers, that were planned or scheduled before the election became pending, may continue, but no new appearances should be arranged during the election period. The same applies to appearances in programmes in a subsidiary capacity, for example, as non-starring compère or sports commentator or as one of a number of participants in a programme outside the field of political or industrial controversy and not relating to current public policy.

> (ITC Programme Code, Appendix 3 –
> Programmes at the time of elections, 8ii)

As you can see, we adhered to that implicitly. It adds:

All other appearances should cease; this includes principal participation by a candidate in any type of non-fictional programme.

> (ibid.)

When in doubt, refer to the relevant guidelines.

Doctors can be contacted via the British Medical Association who are happy to help. For something more specific such as a neurosurgeon, the Royal College of Surgeons will give you the name of the Society in whose specialism you are interested. The Royal College of Physicians will put you on to a neurologist and so on. The main Colleges are in London but the Scottish Colleges are based in Edinburgh and Glasgow.

The nearest hospital might help; you might even try your GP and don't forget contacts within your own programme team. Be warned, doctors are extremely busy and most need advance notice.

*Lawyers* are contactable via the Law Society.

I am lumping together *academics* and other professionals like astronomers and historians and sociologists. Universities and colleges, the Royal Observatory at Greenwich, specific professional associations, all can be contacted for leads (see Chapter 3). Finding an expert is relatively easy but their televisual and radio quality can be hit and miss. The reason for the same face or voice cropping up time and again is because the production team are playing safe, well aware that their expert will perform to order and give good value. It may be seen as lazy but it is also expedient.

When an expert is wanted *now*, the contacts book is crucial. Note the name and expertise of each contributor with their numbers (mobile, home, *direct line* at work, e-mail, fax) and file it away.

There are associations, charities and agencies (refer to Chapter 3) for virtually everything and these are invaluable for spokespersons from the world of business through to self-help groups.

Payment for contributors depends entirely on the budget, the type of programme and the form of contribution. Experts expect their travel expenses to be covered (unless the programme provides a taxi) and a payment around the £50–£100 mark. They may ask for more. The BBC fees have been set, at the time of writing, at the lower end of this figure. Politicians and the like (spokespersons for news items) are not paid.

## DOCUMENTARIES

The main difference between someone appearing on a half-hour chat show and taking part in a similar length documentary is that a documentary takes considerably longer to film. Anyone appearing in a documentary gives up a lot of their time, potentially exposes themselves to the world and has more to gain – or lose.

A documentary is, by its very nature, supposed to document reality. This is not the place for a media debate on the issues of reality except to confirm that most documentary makers try their utmost to present the truth as they see it.

It is important that the programme team do not impose their own viewpoint over the opinions of the contributors. Nor should they intentionally misinterpret or misrepresent what people say (refer to BSC codes of conduct).

It is surprisingly common for production crews to get personally involved in the lives of their subjects although, in the majority of cases, this happens with emotional topics or when documentaries are filmed over several months. During the filming of a series about couples undergoing fertility treatment, a producer/director found herself pregnant and agonised about revealing this to the women who were now part of her daily life. Professionally speaking, perhaps programme makers should draw a line between themselves and their documentary subjects. In some extraordinary way you must be prepared for an umbilical cord making you feel responsible for how someone comes across on screen and their subsequent welfare. I kept in touch with a family in Yorkshire for years after the miners' strike and received letters for ages about his family life from a fifteen-year-old lad I once auditioned (and turned down).

For documentaries, meeting the people beforehand is mandatory. What do they look like? Do they talk well? Are they nervous? Will the audience feel attuned and sympathetic to them?

It is virtually impossible to know beforehand how well someone will work on television. Their confidence and how articulate they are at the initial meeting is a good indicator but fallible. I have met wonderful people who fell apart when the camera was pointed at them and others, initially shy and reticent, who came across on camera as quietly confident and well-informed. Usually, however, the initial gut feeling is an accurate indicator.

Finding people in the first place depends on the type of documentary and its topic. If it is based on a situation such as a driving school, trawl through several driving schools, getting speculative permission first. It is a bit chicken and egg – does one get permission to film first or find suitable people? There is no hard and fast answer, it depends on the circumstances.

When 'casting', meet more people than you intend to film so that you can whittle down the unsuitable ones and have reserves for those who back out.

Again, aim for a variety of age, class, race and gender. The types represented by the Spice Girls and other manufactured groups are an example of somebody for everybody. Try not to fill the programme with eccentrics but involve a few 'normal' people as well. The major ingredient of a docu-soap is the people and their stories and this is what makes them work. Avoid stereotypes although it could be argued that they make for a better programme; the audience likes having its prejudices confirmed but sociologists and critics question the use of stereotypes in television, and docu-soaps in particular.

Visit prospective contributors in their own setting. If they are comfortable in their own surroundings, this gives a better idea to their personality and reaction to appearing on television. It also offers an insurance policy to validate their identity and corroborate the honesty clause should one be required.

Never promise anything at this stage but warn them when filming is likely to be and how long it might take. Potentially are they free? Be realistic. Filming takes longer than they imagine, is hard work and a lot of commitment.

Why do people commit themselves to being filmed? The 'this will change my life and make me famous' idea is a major reason for signing up for a year on a tropical island or having every minute of the day recorded for three months in a 'social experiment'. For some it worked. Jane McDonald of *Cruise* is a good example. Maureen Rees from *Driving School*, Jeremy Spake from *Airport*, Trude Mostue from *Vets in Practice* and subsequent series have become celebrities in their own right. Maureen Rees was taken on the books of an agent, thus putting her on the celebrity circuit. These are exceptions. Most people who take part in a documentary are never heard of again in media terms, although it may change their life in ways which we, the viewer, do not know about.

A researcher, however, must be aware that anyone taking part in a documentary risks, as a consequence, their marriage breaking down, their business folding or losing their job. But it is not entirely the researcher or television itself that should bear the brunt of the responsibility. The people taking part are not entirely innocent bystanders. It is, however, the programme makers' responsibility to ensure that the subjects know what they are letting themselves in for and that their life may be inadvertently changed and not necessarily for the better. The Broadcasting Standards Commission gives advice on what you must tell a contributor before recording.

For further information, tips and details on organising filming with contributors refer to Chapter 8, filming on location.

## CHILDREN

Most children love the idea of appearing on television. For a one-off event, a Saturday morning children's programme for instance, great – the child isn't taking time off school. However, there are still regulations to be considered.

- Children under 16 must be chaperoned by an adult, usually a parent. If several children are coming from the same school, depending on the number, one teacher can accompany them. Legally, however, if a child (or children) is accompanied to the studio by anyone other than a parent, parental permission must be sought in writing beforehand.

- Chaperones (other than parents) must be approved by the Local Education Authority. Teachers, of course, are already licensed by the LEA.

- For time off school, the head teacher must grant permission. Very often, a parent is prepared to approach them for you. Head teachers tend to consider a pupil appearing on television as educational but in the current climate against parentally-condoned truancy, the head teacher *must* give authorisation prior to recording.

- According to Equity rules, if a child actor or model is working, the chaperone is a professional and will be paid. This applies even to parents.

Other considerations:

- check beforehand what they intend to wear and suggest they bring a change of clothes in case their choice is unsuitable. Children are more likely than adults to insist on wearing sweatshirts emblazoned with commercial logos (e.g. Nike, Adidas) and must be encouraged to wear something else, however unfashionable it might appear to their friends;

- as a rule of thumb, children under 16 appearing as themselves and not acting in a drama do not require makeup. The makeup department prefer to make the final decision;

- remind them to go to the loo first.

Child employment is heavily regulated and a child acting in a drama must be licensed by their Local Education Authority. The Casting Department usually oversees this and are well aware of the current legislation governing child actors insofar as the number of hours a day they are permitted to work.

Some Local Education Authorities interpret the rules very strictly, insisting all children in their area are licensed even for one day off school. In my experience this rarely happens but I have come across it. To obtain a licence, three weeks' notice should be given. Any less than this and it depends on the LEA as to whether they can process the licence in time. Some are more accommodating than others but it may simply come down to how stretched they are in the office.

One of the licence requirements is that a child missing more than a certain number of days from school has a tutor but, apart from soap or feature film actors, these are rare. As with the chaperone, the tutor must be approved by the Local Education Authority. The Casting Department can recommend one. Both chaperones and tutors need somewhere to wait whilst the pupil is on set. This may be as simple as a chair at the back of the studio or even next to them in the audience. For children with a tutor, a suitable room must be supplied for schoolwork for when the child is not required on set. This is usually a dressing room or the green room.

For further guidance on working with children, contact the Local Education Authority, Equity and the Casting Department. The regulatory bodies' guidelines are also useful.

## PERSUADING SOMEONE TO BE FILMED

It occasionally happens that someone has a particularly pertinent story or viewpoint but is unhappy or unwilling to be filmed. Media folk are ambitious, persuasive, tenacious and implacable; you need to be sure of the reasons why someone is hesitant before bullying them into appearing. The ethical implications are enormous.

There may be a number of reasons for their reluctance:

- they have been in a traumatic or deeply personal situation and don't want to bring back the memory especially in front of an audience of millions;

- they do not want to be recognised;

- they have been mistreated or misrepresented by the media in the past;

- they do not think their story is important enough;

- they are afraid of making a fool of themselves.

All the regulatory guidelines are specific about approaching the extremely distressed. Under the 'Privacy, Gathering of Information' section, if you persist with someone in this position, you *must* ensure your actions are justified within the remit of the programme code.

For those who do not wish to be recognised can you justify persuading them to take part if they are putting themselves into physical danger? Should someone coming out as gay be faced later with parental ostracism and the subsequent emotional turmoil? How would you feel if, by appearing on television, what you were terrified of materialised?

Many media professionals, in order to persuade someone to appear, promise anonymity by making the contributor unrecognisable. The most common method is to record the person under low lights or in silhouette. This cannot be guaranteed and not necessarily because of lack of integrity from the director or cameraman's part. I have seen films where a director has recorded under low light or in silhouette but when the item reached telecine, the operator forced up the light levels until the person was totally recognisable. In his opinion, the exposure was of non-broadcast quality. Alternatively, film the person facing away from camera. If the light levels are raised, only the back of the head can be seen. It is by no means fail-safe; hair colour and style is recognisable to anyone in the know, as is the other approach of filming extreme close ups of mouth and eyes.

Voice disguise is another option. Although people feel less vulnerable appearing on radio, they still occasionally request anonymity and voice disguise is an added security on television too. To do this, complete cooperation with the sound department is required and it must be explained on air and in the voiceover that the voice has been intentionally distorted.

Being mistreated or misrepresented by the media in the past is a common reason for being turned down. I know how the media operates and I have turned down programme appearances, even when offered a fee.

A rural headmaster once refused me permission to film his pupils. Apparently, a film crew had filmed there a year or two previously and, because no-one had explained the filming procedure (I hesitate to use the words 'misrepresented' or 'lied') the children had re-enacted the same shots over and over again until they were cold, hungry, in tears and hours late for school. He was understandably angry and upset. I commiserated, cajoled and sweet-talked my way, speaking to many of the parents (it was a small school) and finally persuaded him to let us film. The director and crew were warned to shoot as quickly and economically as possible. A bouquet of flowers, for what it was worth, was dispatched with the facility fee and thank-you letter.

An arrogant and mob-handed attitude can do untold damage to the general perception of film making, especially if there is little prior information of the processes involved. Filming takes a long time, and for those being filmed it can be boring. It always has been and it always will.

For those people who turn down taking part because they don't think their story is important enough, you must rely on persuasion. The offer of a fee may help. The same applies for those who don't want to be filmed because they are afraid of making a fool of themselves. In my experience, these are the hardest to persuade and you may have to concede failure. Some producers don't take kindly to this. My attitude is pragmatic. If someone is persuaded against their will, the most likely outcome is that they will be dreadful and you may as well have given up gracefully in the first place, as well as possibly contravening the BSC's code of conduct.

On the other hand, most people are only too willing to talk to the cameras.

## Doorstepping

This is the practice of turning up unannounced with a camera or sound recorder and demanding someone speaks to you while you film; *The Cook Report* is a typical exponent, as are the paparazzi who stalk houses for a photograph or sound bite. It goes without saying they probably don't want to be filmed. Apart from current affairs programmes and the news, researchers are rarely expected to do this. The main considerations are one of ethics (privacy) and safety. Irate victims tend to take offence. There is new legislation at White Paper level which may restrict doorstepping in the future or make it illegal. For current codes of practice about doorstepping, refer to the BSC.

## STUDIO PRACTICE

### Minding guests

During production, a researcher often acts in the role of host or hostess minding contestants, celebrities, experts and whoever is involved. In the early days of television, the call-boy (a young lad or girl in their first television job) accompanied actors between dressing room, makeup and wardrobe and onto the set. Nowadays, apart from the occasional assistant stage manager working on a large production, the researchers do it. Together with dollops of tact for nervous guests, the researcher must be familiar with the studio set up and the location of makeup and wardrobe departments. They must also be aware of the recording schedule so that their charges are not late on the studio floor. If a guest has brought personal props or photographs, the researcher ensures the props are safe and the photographs sent to the correct department for recording onto a suitable format. If in doubt which department, the floor manager or director will know. As the floor manager is probably more approachable during recording day, check with them rather than the director who is likely to be fraught up in the control room.

For anyone expecting travel expenses or an appearance fee, the researcher must obtain a float in advance. Payment may, however, be the responsibility of the production assistant or the Casting Department.

Always obtain a receipt to clear the float.

### Background notes for presenters and producers

The presenter/interviewer and producer need to know what each contributor, contestant or expert is likely to say. Biographies of celebrity guests for background information may also be required. What nobody wants, and hasn't time or inclination to read, is thirty pages of closely written information:

- half a side of A4 should (depending on the programme) be sufficient;
- bullet points will do.

## Information sources for background notes and what to include

- *Celebrities:* the agent or manager, cuttings library, publisher, etc., will provide short biographies and a list of credits. These can be précised into short notes but may already be concise enough.

- *Experts: Who's Who* (a directory of influential people still living) may have your guest listed alongside their date of birth, status, education, publications, hobbies and other useful information.

- *Contributors making short points on a daytime chat show:* the initial phone call. Their name (correctly spelt) and a summary (two or three lines maximum) should suffice.

- A cuttings service (Chapter 3) is a useful source for background information but may perpetuate inaccuracies.

Occasionally it is worth including guidance questions to lead the presenter more quickly to the guest's anecdote.

## Talk back system

Researchers are wired to the talk back system so that they are aware of what is happening in the studio and the control room (where the producer, director, vision mixer, etc., are during recording) and are immediately contactable.

Rarely does a researcher find themselves in the studio control room (also known as the gallery or box depending on the television station) during recording. More often, they are found on the studio floor or running (walking purposefully ...) between the dressing rooms, makeup, wardrobe and green room (the waiting area named after theatre green rooms traditionally painted green to relieve the glare from the stage lights).

In quiz programmes the score system is often operated from the studio floor and one of the researchers is assigned the task of supervising and double-checking the scores.

## AND AFTERWARDS ...

### Thank-you letters and transmission (tx) dates

It is a matter of courtesy to thank contributors both when they leave the recording session and in a follow-up letter. Contributors are always desperate to know when they will be 'on telly' and if you know the transmission date, the follow-up letter can confirm it. If by chance, and it happens quite frequently, the tx date changes, a quick phone call will do wonders for the credibility and good will of the station.

An alternative way of letting people know tx dates is in permission release forms or letter confirming their appearance. Even if the date is unconfirmed, the production office should have a vague idea. 7 p.m. on Tuesdays from February is far more helpful than 'sometime next year'. Because production schedules are so frantic, this removes the burden of phoning everyone up especially as, by transmission, the production team are likely to be working on different projects.

## VHS copies

Contributors often request VHS copies giving the excuse they are away on holiday, they forgot it was on, they live outside the transmission area. Few TV stations make provision for this service; a commonly given reason is that if everyone who asked for a copy got one there'd be no time to make programmes. Another is that the cumulative cost of tapes and engineers' time is too much. A final reason, of course, is one of copyright. By letting people know the tx time and warning them in advance that VHS copies cannot be made, the request is averted beforehand.

An exception is if

> a person or organisation can establish a reasonable claim that something derogatory has been broadcast about them, or that they are affected by alleged criticism, unfairness or inaccuracy, and request a recording or transcript, it should normally be provided.
>
> (*ITC Programme Code: 11.* Communication with the Public 11.2 (ii)
> Programme recordings and transcripts, Provision to others)

The ITC code continues to say that a letter of explanation or apology may be more appropriate and that, if legal advice has been sought, sending out a recording or transcript may be delayed. In other words, if the programme has had serious allegations made against it, which is why a copy has been requested, the producer will already be seeking advice from the lawyers.

## PERSONAL SAFETY

There are some strange people out there and ambitious media people want to make interesting programmes. This invariably means working on weird, bizarre, sensational, controversial and, at times, downright dangerous ideas. When working on programmes about crime or the abnormal, the researcher is putting him or herself at risk and personal safety is a serious issue. The media industry is increasingly concerned with risk assessment and avoiding potential problems. Taking precautions is advisable before meeting new people. Bearing in mind that the most dangerous situations are unpredictable, anyone genuine will appreciate and understand the need for such precautions.

- Always let someone in your production team know where you are going and whom you are meeting.

- Leave the phone number of where you are meeting them with a colleague.

- Take a mobile phone, leave it on whilst away from the office but don't use it when driving.

- Meet in a public place, which may not be possible if you are meeting them at their house, place of work or assessing filming on location. Please refer to Chapter 8.

- When in doubt take someone with you – e.g. a fellow researcher or the director.

- Work out the route before you leave. Fussing with an A–Z on a major road is asking for trouble.

- Ensure your car is roadworthy and there is sufficient petrol. Your car should be insured for business use.

- Leave with plenty of time so that you are not stressed and flurried.

These are basic precautions. Neither this nor any other book can prepare you for the unexpected.

## SUMMARY

- There is no 'one-stop' place to find contributors.

- Double-check all arrangements.

- Whenever possible, get direct-line phone numbers to save going through switchboard.

- Take note of gut feelings of something being wrong. You are usually right.

- Refer to the BSC codes of conduct about dealing fairly with contributors.

# 5
# Pictures, photographs and film clips

At some time in their career, most researchers deal with pictures, photographs and film clips. For the television researcher, it may be mainly visual – archive news clips, photographs of an ageing Hollywood actress in her heyday, a family photo, a clip from a feature film. The radio researcher may locate sound archives and film and television clips with sound tracks suitable for broadcast.

The most important consideration is that of copyright. Whatever you use, the chance is that someone somewhere owns the rights to the material.

Who owns the rights? The source of the photographs, films and pictures will often help but do not assume, however, that the source itself is the only owner of the rights. In some cases, you may have to pay two fees or more.

The reproduction cost depends on the broadcast area and how many times it will be shown. For non-broadcast material, i.e. corporate use, the royalty payments are usually less than for transmission. As a rule of thumb, the greater the potential audience, the higher the charge.

## PHOTOGRAPHS AND PICTURES

Photographs, paintings, lithographs, drawings and other visuals add an extra dimension to a TV programme and are used everywhere from quizzes and chat shows to biographies, current affairs, the news, documentaries and dramas.

The most uncomplicated photographs to find and use are those supplied and owned by a contributor or contestant; the snapshot taken by mum of daughter ten years ago. The contributor took the photograph, owns the copyright and by supplying it, tacitly gives permission to use it. It is doubtful that they will expect payment for the use of the photo and everyone is happy with the arrangement.

It gets a little more complicated when someone else took the photograph, for instance a wedding photo. Technically, the copyright is with the original photographer even though the bride and groom understandably assume that, because the photograph is of them and they commissioned the photos in the first place, they own it. It is a frustrating exercise seeking out the photographer for permission, especially when there is little time. Many researchers take the expedient and pragmatic approach that most photographers won't remember an individual wedding anyway. This seems reasonable but repercussions can result in an unbudgeted expense and you, the researcher, will be deemed responsible.

Another presumption is that, because copyright lasts 70 years after the death of the originator of the work, paintings like Leonardo da Vinci's *Mona Lisa* is out of copyright and the picture can be reproduced on screen without incurring a fee. Wrong.

Firstly, one needs a photograph or transparency of it. The photographer owns the copyright of the photograph and expects a fee. An alternative is to send a crew to film it at the Louvre in Paris. Not only must the crew be paid, the Louvre will charge a facility fee for filming it. The cheapest and simplest method is to use the original idea – the slide or photograph and pay the photographer. With luck, the television station already has a slide or photo taken by a staff photographer for a previous programme . . .

## Copyright

Copyright laws change regularly and it is such a complicated issue that some law firms specialise in it. This, therefore, is a brief guideline to point you away from making simple but expensive mistakes. If in doubt, talk to your rights department for advice.

In the Duration of Copyright and Rights in Performances Regulations 1995, the copyright protection afforded by the Copyright Designs and Patents Act 1988 was extended to 'life plus 70 years'.

Another big change occurred in 1996 when 'the Term Directive' allowed the copyright to be retained by freelance photographers, even those whose work was commissioned. The rights to use their photographs have to be negotiated. In effect, this is why the photographer who took the wedding photos retains the copyright.

For photographers employed full-time by a commercial company, the copyright to their photographs belongs to the company and the photographer's salary, the stock and processing costs are met by them. The copyright of photos shot for use in specific programmes and for promotional purposes, if taken by staff employees, belong to the production company and are ostensibly free.

## Photograph and picture libraries

The main source for photographs and pictures are libraries and photographic agencies.

In a large television station the first phone call is to the *in-house photo library* which may provide what you want. If the station owns the copyright, there is no royalty payment. For photos and pictures they store but for which the copyright is held elsewhere, the librarians should have the copyright owner's name written on the back and it is a simple step to negotiate reproduction permission and the fee. For unfamiliar names or an obsolete phone number, a call to BAPLA (British Association of Picture Libraries and Agencies) may be able to provide an up-to-date contact.

Unfortunately, in-house picture libraries are of limited value as they are restricted to production stills or material for use in programmes that have little bearing on the new topic. For BBC researchers this may not be the case, because the BBC Photograph Library dates back to 1924. The library is run as a commercial enterprise and everyone pays a charge for using the facility. For those working on BBC productions there is a nominal internal costing charge.

*Commercial libraries and agencies* exist to make money from the photographs held in their possessions and the largest contain thousands of photographs taken by a wide range of freelance photographers who own the rights to their own work. Both the agency and the photographer earn money when photographs are reproduced in books, magazines, newspapers or on television. The agency supplies photographs and pays the photographer a certain percentage from the commission, usually 50 per cent.

Libraries specialise. One may hold collections based on geography, another sport, action shots, people, natural history and so on. Some specialise in archive material and here you will find lithographs and prints from books instead of photos, although they might house a few of these by default. This is useful for visual material before the advent of photography. *The Mary Evans Picture Library* is an example. *The Kobal Collection* specialises in cinema and television, and holds paraphernalia such as film posters and fan magazines. The Press Association News photo library specialises in photos which made the newspapers from the 1890s to today.

## Locating picture libraries and agencies

The governing body for picture libraries and agencies is the British Association of Picture Libraries and Agencies (BAPLA) and it publishes a list of its 400-plus members. The website, www.bapla.org.uk, has a search facility which means that, by typing in the requirement, e.g. 'butterflies', a list of all their members holding pictures and photographs of butterflies will be revealed.

Lists of the larger agencies are also published in:

- *The Guardian Media Guide*;

- *Writers' and Artists' Yearbook*;

- *The Writer's Handbook*;

- *The Picture Researcher's Handbook* by Hilary and Mary Evans (from the eponymous picture library). This is extremely specialised and lists libraries and other sources worldwide;

- *The Knowledge* (see under 'stills libraries').

Agencies are usually contacted by phone; the researcher rings through a request and the agency sends out examples of what they have by post or e-mail. The researcher will choose a selection before obtaining the original. Visits are strictly by appointment.

At the time of writing, digital photography, although extremely important in the print industry where speed is crucial, has not fully infiltrated the world of television. Instead, a transparency ('tranny') or good quality print is more likely to be requested by the graphics department because of the versatile format and, on the whole, better quality. This may change over the next few years.

However, examples of photos and pictures can now be downloaded digitally, and it is less common for agencies to post batches of original trannies and photographs from which the researcher can make the final choice. This was a hazardous practice for irreplaceable material. Today, the researcher makes the final choice from catalogues (printed or downloaded via the Internet or e-mail) and only the master copy of slides and photographs is physically despatched. As digital quality improves, even this practice may soon cease.

## Compensation for loss of material

Many of these items are unique and irreplaceable, and a stiff penalty is incurred should any material be lost or damaged on return. The compensation is in the realm of £500 or more per article (at the time of writing) and a member of the production team need only lose one transparency for this to be a considerable strain on the budget. For researchers working with material from picture and photograph libraries, it is crucial to organise a system for their safekeeping and return. Insurance, recorded mail systems or couriers are essential.

## Flash fees

The usual payment for reproducing photographs and other copyrighted pictures is the 'flash fee' (a reproduction or licence fee for the use of the images). The overall cost of the licence depends on how long the photograph is 'flashed' on screen and how many times the programme is likely to be repeated.

The standard payment is a set fee for the first flash lasting a stipulated period of time, usually 30 seconds. A repeat flash within the same episode is normally a percentage of the first fee, commonly 50 per cent. The cost itself depends on the source. There is no standard fee although most agencies charge around £75 for the first flash but may charge more. Deals can be struck if a photograph is used several times in a series or if the agency supplies a large amount of pictures.

According to Glen Marks of Rex Features, television companies nowadays send out blanket permission forms which, once signed, give unlimited use of the pictures (including promotions and trailers) for a particular programme. Picture agencies are understandably unhappy about this and often cross through the relevant clauses. Whereas I understand the television company covering itself, my sympathy lies with the photographer often earning little in a precarious profession.

## Clearing copyright

The method by which permission is sought for the use of photographs (and music, see Chapter 7) is called 'clearing copyright'.

For pictures and photos it is a simple procedure. The agency providing the photos sends a form (effectively the licence) that is either completed by the PA or anyone else taking the responsibility and includes how long each picture was featured on screen. It is usual for the fees to be paid after transmission although permission *must* be sought prior to reproduction (i.e. recording). Some agencies, being small commercial concerns, have cash-flow problems and may insist on the fees being paid within three months of supplying the pictures.

Agencies pay the photographers who supplied the photos so it is important for the researcher to jot down the reference number of the photo used in the programme. If you just say to the agency, 'We used ten of your photos' the agency won't know who to pay.

## Onscreen credits

It is not a legal requirement to credit individual photographers onscreen, although as a matter of courtesy their names are printed in newspapers, books and magazines, especially when the photograph is of high aesthetic and technical quality. It is, however, common for agencies to be credited at the end of television programmes, especially when a large amount of their material is used within the series. They may well insist.

Photographers have the right to object to their photographs being distorted or mutilated if they consider it damages their reputation.

## The Internet

Downloading samples of material from agencies via the Internet is a useful research tool but no material found on it is copyright free – certainly nothing supplied by photographic agencies. Pathé News, for example, is planning to put samples of their material on the Internet intended for downloading by students on media courses. For broadcast use, royalties must still be paid. A search on the Internet may throw up a useful production still from a film. By contacting the distribution company direct it may be possible to use it royalty free if it is promoting the film. *Promotion* is only possible before general release and for a short period immediately afterwards. The distribution company will provide a good quality print and inform you of the copyright holder if it isn't them.

There is also a quality issue. Material reproduced from the Internet is not of broadcast quality, although that might change over the next few years.

By all means, use the Internet for inspiration and ideas, and for downloading samples from agencies, but the official body still needs to be contacted.

## FILM AND TELEVISION CLIPS

It is a common assumption that a documentary consisting almost entirely of archive footage is cheap to produce. After all, it's 'only a load of old films' (for sound archives, see Chapter 10). Unfortunately, nothing could be further from the truth and compilation programmes using a large amount of old footage are extremely expensive. There are several reasons for this, finding unique or hitherto little-seen material is expensive in research time and royalty fees do not come cheap. Clips from feature films do not make 'cheap telly' either.

When programmes use large amounts of library footage, it is common to contract *specialist film researchers*, often on a freelance basis. A few large companies employ specialist film researchers to be consulted in-house by anyone needing expert help. Clipsalesnow.com may well change all this (see p. 77).

When a researcher working for one of these companies needs film clips, it is protocol to contact the film researcher. By explaining the request to them, the time scale and any other requirements, the film researcher will find an assort-ment of clips from which the production team can make the final choice. Copyright details and fees, together with their time (which is part of an internal costing system) will be charged against the programme budget. From you, the film researcher will request a programme or production number against which they will charge the incidental expenses.

Film research incurs costs more than just the royalty payment including (depending on the source of the film) service charges, handling fees, the cost of the viewing copy, the videotape and dubbing charges. These are explained later.

If there is no specialist film researcher, the job falls to you.

A word of warning; unless the brief is relatively simple, a few shots of Paris, say, or a snatch from a recent feature film for a celebrity interview, money and stress may be saved in the long term by employing a film research company. Check their charges before consulting the producer. Simple briefs should be easy because this is how film libraries make their profits.

Where you start depends on what you want. Remember the curse: 'It'll only take an hour' always takes a lot longer!

## Locating film clips/stock shots and archive footage

For researchers working for a large television company, the first stop is always the in-house film and video library. There is no problem with access or copy-right unless the material contains footage brought in from elsewhere and the librarians will forewarn you of this. Internal costing systems, however, are common and the programme budget will incur the same incidental costs as they would elsewhere (dubbing fees, for instance). You will be told what can and can't be used and dubious material will not be transferred onto a broad-cast format. Drama can be difficult and this is covered later.

*Stock shots* are general film clips such as a beach scene, woods, Blackpool Tower and so on. They are too short and insignificant to warrant employing a video crew for a whole day. For stock shots, again, it is worth going to the in-house video or film library and asking if they have anything suitable. Once they have located a selection of shots, they can be viewed and a selection made. In my experience, stock shots kept by in-house video libraries are disap-pointing and there is a compromise between cost and quality. Cost usually wins. If the stock shots are really not good enough, then the next stop is the commercial stock shot library. This is similar to an in-house stock shot library except that you pay commercial rates for the footage. These rates are still con-siderably cheaper than employing a video crew.

## News archives

News footage comes from a variety of sources. Before the advent of television, the main news source was the press and the wireless but an important visual source was the cinema newsreel, an important element of cinema-going until the late 1960s.

British Pathé News is perhaps the most famous of the cinema newsreels. Their footage dates from 1895 until 1970 when newsreels were superseded by television. British Movietone News has material from 1929 to 1979.

For other sources of news footage, ITN (who also manage Reuters, Paramount, NBC and some BBC but not sport footage), and the BBC are the most obvious. ITN has its database on line at www.itnarchive.com and by referring to the shot lists a decision can be made as to which shots to order up. It is also possible to order up a VHS viewing tape first at a cost of £100 to cover research, dubbing and tape costs. The viewing tape charge must be paid even if no clips are chosen. Other companies will send out viewing tapes on request but, again, there will be a charge for it. Regional stations such as Granada, Anglia, Central and Scottish also have libraries. Most libraries will let you view their footage on site by appointment.

For foreign news sources, I strongly advise commissioning a specialist film researcher although ITN Archive and the BBC have stringers (freelance contributor paid by the item, often a journalist or cameraman) working around the world and may have relevant footage. The main problem with foreign material is one of copyright and, although the BBC and ITN footage will have notes about the rights holders, it may be extremely difficult and onerous to clear.

## Sporting events

Sport is big business and companies around the world negotiate for the rights to own, screen and sponsor sporting events which makes the broadcast clearance extremely complicated. The rights to broadcasting Wimbledon, the Olympics, cricket and, until the last few years, the major football matches in the UK were all in the domain of the BBC. However, in April 2000, in a blaze of publicity ITV won the rights to transmit the *Match of the Day* Premier League highlights, although the BBC regained live FA Cup Final rights from ITV. On the other hand, the BBC was awarded the television rights to Wimbledon from 2000 for the next five years although Video Networks had the video-on-demand rights to Wimbledon and major matches from the next day. To justify the billions that the exclusive rights cost, the broadcast companies must recoup their investment *and* make a profit.

The result is that, once you have located the footage, you may have to pay twice, once to the footage copyright holder and also to the holder of the event. To make it more complicated, depending on the event and where the item is to be transmitted, there may be more than one rights holder.

A simple example is the Olympics. A payment is required to the owner of the clip you want to use and a second payment is made to the IOC (International Olympics Committee).

On the whole, though, once you have located the required footage, the source of that clip should have information on where to go to clear the rights. It is the responsibility of the company requiring the footage to ensure that all clearance is carried out correctly. That may be you. Depending on the age of the clip it may not be straightforward.

The cost of using clips from sporting events can mount up and, for programmes with low budgets, be prohibitive.

Notwithstanding the problems of locating and paying for the reproduction rights, there may be other reasons why the footage cannot be used. The BBC, for instance, vetoes the use of clips from certain sporting events because of the amount of integral advertising. In Formula 1 racing, not only are the advertisements highly visible around the circuit but the cars themselves are plastered with the logos of sponsorship companies.

## Royalties for news footage

Once a clip has been chosen, unless the company has a credit account with them, ITN Archive insists royalty payments are paid up front before they send the broadcast-quality Beta tape.

Footage is paid by the amount used and there is a minimum charge. For British Pathé News the minimum is 25 seconds (or part thereof) and for ITN Archive, it is a minute (or part thereof). The BBC would expect to pay a royalty charge of approximately £489 (at the time of writing) for a clip lasting a minute or under from ITN Archive for one transmission on a UK broadcast or £735 unlimited. ITV and Channel 4 companies get a 40 per cent discount because ITN supplies them with their news and their royalty fee is £294 per minute for a single broadcast or £441 unlimited. Like picture libraries, deals can be struck if a large amount of footage is to be used.

Whichever source news footage comes from, the total royalty levied depends on how much is used, what it is used for (i.e. television, feature films, adverts, corporate videos), the transmission area, the number of transmissions and the length of the licence (five/ten years or in perpetuity is common). On the sliding scale, feature films pay the most. British Pathé News charges (at the time of writing) £120 per second (minimum charge 25 seconds) for footage to be included in a feature film 'in perpetuity'. There are lower charges for museum displays and other charges for CD Roms, the Internet, pop promos and advertising. For television rights, there is another scale, again with a minimum charge of 25 seconds for one country, one transmission and one specified programme. The more countries the programme is sold to, the higher the rate. Licences apply for a fixed term, say five or ten years, and should the programme be repeated outside this time scale, the rights must be renegotiated.

## Television programmes

Until 1957, British television consisted of one channel, the BBC. Many of the programmes transmitted in the early days of television were live and the only way to record copies was via a system called telerecording whereby a camera literally filmed what was being transmitted via the cathode ray tube. Not only are these copies of an extremely poor quality compared to what we expect today, if copies exist at all, but they are, of course, in black and white. The first colour transmission on British TV was in 1967, although some programmes after this time were still made in monochrome.

For many of the well-loved BBC favourites there are no copies in existence because they were wiped by accident or by over-zealous librarians clearing shelf space. The BBC is so desperate to recover copies of missing episodes that there is an amnesty for the return of illegally-held copies.

Although one imagines that the rights to television programmes belong to the company who made them, this depends partly on whether the television company is still in existence and partly on whether the company has been taken over by another. ITV companies from the early days of television, Rediffusion and ATV for instance, have either disappeared or been taken over. Granada, who first transmitted in 1957, is the only original ITV company retaining its licence. Over recent years it has taken over LWT, Tyne Tees and Yorkshire TV and in July 2000 put in a bid for United Television therefore owning Anglia, Meridian and HTV as well. However, because of the rules of ownership, it is expected that Harlech will be sold to Carlton. Carlton, the other main commercial television company, owns (at the time of writing) Carlton, Central, West Country and (if it buys it from Granada) HTV. There are also a myriad of smaller independent production companies and, for the uninitiated, it is a maze working out who owns what and where one goes for a) copies of the clip required, b) permission to include it and c) who to pay. Effectively, if you want to use a television programme, you need to know who owns the archives.

When contacting the libraries, the more information you can give them, the better. If you know the title of the programme, the transmission date, who was appearing in it, all this will help them locate the footage or at least give you a clue to where to go next.

Again, all this might be about to change with the introduction of Clipsalesnow.com.

## Clipsalesnow.com

In February 2001, Clipsalesnow.com was set up to simplify the archive market and make money from it. The on-line sales rights to various libraries and broadcasters were signed up, the archives transferred into a digital format and a searchable index on a free-to-access website was provided at www.clipsalesnow.com. Researchers type in key words, view the footage at no extra cost and order it up on-line in whatever format is required. The clips, at the time of writing, would cost from £400 to £5,000 per minute depending on the transmission area and the length of the licence. Whether or not Clipsalesnow.com revolutionises the market and simplifies the use of archives remains to be seen.

## Television drama

Acting is a notoriously precarious and impecunious profession – a household name this year may never be heard of again. Those few actors earning a living wage this year may work in a burger restaurant next.

Actors' contracts state how many times the programme may be repeated within a set time limit and after this has expired, any repeat fees paid depends on the initial agreement. Using extracts from television drama can be complicated and the payment depends on the original agreement. There is also a need, in certain cases, for the performer to consent before the extract can be broadcast. The following information is taken from the *Equity Television Agreements 2000*.

## Consents for television drama

For a BBC programme to use an extract from a BBC programme:

- Extracts under 4 minutes – no consent required unless performer is a variety or speciality act when the extract is limited to under 2 minutes (without prior permission). The extract mustn't show the whole act or the climax.

- Extracts criticising or ridiculing the artist's performance or featuring full-frontal nudity or are explicitly sexual – consent required.

If a non-BBC programme wants to use a BBC extract:

- consent is required and a BBC extract rate would be payable.

In ITV programmes, a similar system applies. For ITV programmes using extracts from other ITV programmes:

- extracts are not to exceed 4 minutes;

- consents are not required for programmes of an instructional, critical, magazine, educational or similar programme;

- consents *are* required for a drama or production not mentioned above;

- extracts criticising or ridiculing the artists' performance or featuring full-frontal nudity or are explicitly sexual – consent required;

For the use of ITV extracts in non-ITV programmes:

- consent is required and an extract rate would be payable.

For PACT productions made by independent production companies commissioned by Channel 4, Channel 5, ITV and the BBC the rules are as follows.

For PACT excerpts to be used in PACT programmes:

- extracts of between 1 and 4 minutes' duration, consent not required if the extracts are to be used in an instructional, critical, magazine, educational or similar programme;

- for extracts used in a drama or programme not mentioned above – consent required;

- extracts criticising or ridiculing the artists' performance or featuring full-frontal nudity or are explicitly sexual – consent required.

## Consent for compilation programmes

A compilation programme is one largely made up of extracts from previously transmitted programmes; the *Best of the Soaps* or a biography of a well-loved artiste. The current consent agreements are as follows:

- BBC – consents not required and no limit to duration;

- ITV – no specific provision but currently the ITV companies must obtain Equity's consent and they will only agree if the individual artistes give their permission. This is soon to change and consents will be required as part of the agreement;

- PACT – for programmes consisting predominately of extracts from programmes transmitted under the PACT agreement, consents are required.

These agreements may change, so consult the casting department or Equity for updates.

## Extract rates

These are the fees paid to artistes when a short clip from something previously transmitted is used on another programme. It is this, together with the royalty payment, which adds up when excerpts are used elsewhere. Although BBC programmes using BBC excerpts do not have to pay royalty fees (similarly Granada programmes using Granada clips, etc.) they still have to pay extract fees to the performers appearing in the clip. For non-BBC programmes using clips from BBC programmes, they have to pay both royalty fees for the use of the clip *as well as* extract rates to the performers appearing in the clips. The only bright light on this horizon is that extras and walk-ons do not get paid extract fees as this was included in their original payment.

At the time of writing, the extract fees for BBC for clips not exceeding 1 minute were £31 and for extracts lasting between 1 minute and 4 minutes (5 minutes for schools' programmes), the fee was £58. This is per performer. And, of course, depending on the duration and what the excerpt consists of, consent may be required as well (see above, pp. 77–8). ITV extract fees will be different as each Equity agreement is separate.

In other words, it is all very complicated and you are advised to ask the Casting Department to cost up and negotiate the use of drama clips before including them in a programme.

## Royalties for television dramas and sitcoms

Not only are the actors paid extract rates, but royalties are incurred for reproducing the footage. Depending on the station and the production company, there is a minimum charge of either 30 seconds or 1 minute or part thereof, just as there is in using news or sporting clips. Of course, if the production company owns the rights (a Granada programme using clips from *Coronation Street*, which it makes) there are no royalty payments.

## Feature films

The contact for recent feature films is their distribution company. For older feature films, the use of extracts can be extremely complicated because it may be almost impossible to work out who owns the rights. Unless you are using a new film and the rights are relatively easy to negotiate, I recommend the use of a specialist film researcher.

## Promotion

When using newly-released or pre general release clips, it may be possible to use the material free of charge although there may be a dubbing charge. This is usually the case in programmes like *Film 2001* when film critics review the feature. Chat shows and other programmes occasionally use the same premise. The distributors will demand an on-screen credit.

## Ratings

The broadcast of feature films and television programmes of a more adult nature are given ratings below the age of which the film is not suitable to be viewed. Trailers and the use of excerpts from films must also abide by the ratings so that, for instance, the use of a clip from a '15' rated film may not be suitable for a daytime television programme. This is clearly stated in the *ITC Programme Code* (1 Offence to Good Taste and Decency, Portray of Violence 1.2iv) and the BSC codes.

Moral attitudes change and films classified more than 15 years ago may nowadays be regarded as suitable for transmission earlier than their rating might imply. Clips should still be vetted for their suitability.

## SERVICE CHARGES, HANDLING COSTS AND DUBBING FEES

Film and stock libraries usually charge administration costs to cover staffing costs. British Pathé News, for instance, has:

- a minimum charge for requests involving photocopying, faxing or e-mailing information;

- a charge for the first eight clips on a 60-minute VHS viewing cassette with library numbers and time code in vision and a further charge for more items;

- a handling charge after initial viewing, for preparing library material for transfer to a tape master or film processing;

- a charge for Beta SP master loans for one week. If these master tapes should be lost or damaged, there is a huge compensation penalty fee – master tapes are irreplaceable.

British Pathé is not alone in charging such costs. Television companies have internal costing systems to cover engineers' dubbing time and the cost of the tapes and these charges go on the programme budget. Other costs include courier charges for urgently required archive material.

## Formats

When archive material is sent out, it is important that it is in the correct format for the programme. Old footage can be in a variety of formats from film (35 mm, 16 mm and even 8 mm) to videotape. Many libraries have transferred their footage onto a more accessible and technically friendly format although the original footage in its original format may be stored in specially constructed vaults. The reason for transferring material is simple – the equipment used twenty years ago for 3" videotape is obsolete and there is no space for it in the modern television studio. Viewing material, if required, is sent out on VHS viewing tapes. The researcher should request time code in vision so that they can check the duration of the clips. For broadcast, the required clips are ordered in the required format. Beta is one of the most common but, if unsure, check with the programme director.

## Onscreen credits

It is usually stipulated that archive material has a full onscreen credit often displayed at the end of the programme. It goes without saying that all captions must be spelt correctly. For feature films, the convention is to reveal the onscreen credit whilst the clip is playing. For sporting and other events governed by exclusive television rights, screen credits are also usually displayed during the broadcast of the clip itself. Double-check where the credit should be screened.

## Public domain

Anything no longer under the term of copyright is deemed to be in the public domain; for instance, Shakespeare's plays. However, the typeface, layouts and notes of the Penguin (or any other published edition) version of *Hamlet* is still governed by copyright.

## Pirate copies

Technically, any reproduction produced without permission of a work still in copyright is a pirate copy. As a legitimate television researcher, there is no justification whatsoever to use a pirate copy of a film or music CD. In the extremely unlikely event that you are offered one, theoretically you could be prosecuted for merely handling it. Working in television or radio, there may be occasions when you have access to a legitimate unreleased music CD or a video copy of a film on general release in the US but not in the UK. Just taking a 'quick copy' for your own use without prior permission from the copyright holders is illegal and, if caught, you risk a hefty fine, perhaps imprisonment and, of course, the loss of your job. As for making copies for profit, courts deal very harshly with people convicted of this and you will never work in television or radio again. Film distributors are so scared of pirate copies of unreleased films being circulated that often only one master copy is kept, held in a secure vault.

## SUMMARY

- All pictures and films are subject to copyright and should be cleared beforehand.

- Some films and photographs can take a long time to clear as the copyright owners may be difficult to locate.

## RESOURCES

The film libraries mentioned in this book are:

- ITN Archive, 200 Grays Inn Road, London, WC1X 8XZ, Tel 020 7430 4480, www.itnarchive.co.uk

- British Pathé, 4th Floor, 60 Charlotte Street, London W1P 2AX, Tel 020 7323 0407, www.britishpathe.com

Picture and film libraries (including stock shot libraries) are listed in:

*The Media Guide*

Evans, Hilary and Mary, *Picture Researcher's Handbook*, 5th edn.

*The Knowledge* www.theknowledgeonline.com

*Writers' and Artists' Yearbook.*

*The Whitebook* www.whitebook.co.uk etc.

Also, see Jenny Morgan, *The Film Researcher's Handbook,* Routledge, 1996 (a guide to film sources in North America, Asia, Australasia and Africa).

## ORGANISATIONS

BAPLA (British Association of Picture Libraries and Agencies), 18 Vine Hill, London EC1R 5DX, Tel 020 7713 1780, e-mail bapla@bapla.demon.co.uk. Website: www.bapla.org.uk.

Researcher's Guide to British Film and TV Collections, British Universities Film and Video Council, 77 Well Street, London W1P 3RE, Tel 020 7393 1500, www.bufvc.ac.uk. This is mainly an academic source.

# 6

# Prizes, question setting, props and sets

Procuring props – 'properties', in full – is the official responsibility of the props buyer and the props department via their 'line manager', the set designer (also known as the production designer) who eponymously designs the set, oversees its manufacture (usually off-site) and its construction in studio. So why should this chapter be included?

For researchers working in LE, quizzes, children's programmes and magazines, the producer may request an unusual prop or a specific prize. The person sitting nearest is assigned the job and this is usually the researcher.

A few years ago, a producer devising an off-beat science programme wanted a futuristic set made from *objets trouvées*. His heart was set on aircraft wreckage. The production designer hadn't a clue where to find it but knew I had contacts in the RAF and was in touch with several aircraft museums. Enough aircraft flotsam and jetsam was found for him to be spoilt for choice. I even suggested a sculptor specialising in *objets trouvées* who was contracted as assistant designer. The icing on the cake, as far as the producer was concerned, was that the aircraft wreckage was free; only the transportation came out of his budget.

The magic word is *free*. One of the reasons a producer asks the researcher to find props for the set or prizes is because the Props Department tend to pay for them, either by hiring or buying them outright.

## PRIZES

The rules on the cash value of quiz prizes have changed over the years and, when ITV was regulated by the IBA (since replaced by the ITC), the value of prizes was seriously limited. Now there is virtually no limit; a million pounds has been won in *Who Wants to be a Millionaire?* The prizes on the BBC, funded by licence payers, are considerably cheaper because

> It is inappropriate to spend Licence Fee or Grant in Aid money on prizes of excessive value.
>
> *(BBC Producers' Guidelines*; Chapter 22:
> Game shows and competitions. 5 Prizes)

Now you know why BBC prizes are traditionally so tacky. However, the BBC states that prizes should *normally* be paid for, suggesting why a programme researcher is asked to 'blag' them for free. This practice appears in the independent sector too.

There is no such thing as a free lunch and free prizes will be of low value unless the donor receives something in return.

The researcher is now treading a professional tightrope. The props department may feel undermined and alienated and, depending on what is *promised* to the supplier as to how the prize is seen, the ITC and BBC's regulations may be infringed. If members of the audience cannot wear sweatshirts endorsing commercial products (see Chapter 4), a programme deliberately showing free products on air may easily be in serious breach of the codes of conduct.

> Programmes must never give an assurance that there will be an on-air credit or any publicity in exchange for the donation of a competition prize. Prizes should be described in an informational non promotional manner. The name of the supplier should not normally be given and the brand name should be mentioned only if it is strictly necessary editorially. In such cases only one reference should be made. Television programmes should take all reasonable steps to avoid showing brand logos.
>
> *(BBC Producers' Guidelines*; Chapter 22: Game shows and competitions.
> 6 Donated Prizes)

Fifteen years ago, stage crews masked company logos with gaffer tape. No-one goes to such lengths nowadays (although every effort is ensured that the logos are not overtly picked up on camera) but the concealing of brand logos is taken seriously enough to ensure that cereal packets on shop shelves in soap operas are constantly changed and moved around so programmes cannot be accused of product placement, endorsement or plugging. (Product placement in feature films, of course, is big business.)

The BBC guidelines do not go as far as outright prohibition of free acquisition of prizes but insists only modest donations should be accepted. It adds that if prizes are visits to special events, the programme should pay for travel and accommodation (*BBC Producers' Guidelines*; Chapter 22: Game shows and competitions).

Record companies and marketing agencies constantly send CDs to production offices, especially music programmes, and eventually the office is in danger of being swamped. The easiest and most pleasant way of clearing the office is by offering them as prizes. On independent radio stations, how often does the audience get a chance to win CDs and sweatshirts? For radio and television programmes, an exclusive sweatshirt, music albums and videotapes are a fun (and free) way of rewarding audience loyalty.

The BBC guidelines permit occasional donations of *modest household goods and services* with approval from the department head but the BBC's editorial integrity cannot be compromised. For more guidance, refer to the BBC's website.

## Question setting

In order to win those prizes, there has to be a competition and the BBC does not allow prizes to be won by sheer luck but to quote from the BBC's guidelines:

> should be awarded on the basis of games or questions which are a test of skill, knowledge or judgement appropriate to the participants and the target audience.
>
> *(BBC Producers' Guidelines*; Chapter 22: Game shows and competitions. 1 General)

In other words, for a radio listener to win CDs they can't be the first person to phone in but they can be the first person to phone in and answer a question correctly.

Quizzes usually commission specialists to set the questions and their names are credited at the end of the show. However, a handful of quiz shows specifically employ researchers to write them.

Question writing is a particular skill requiring high attention to detail; a question can't be repeated in the same series and the answers must be correct. Either way, verification is extremely important, both to check the answers are correct and to ensure there is no ambiguity and the possibility of two or more correct answers. For this reason, most quiz programmes contract separate question verifiers to double-check accuracy. If a contestant queries an answer on camera, it is a common procedure to refer to the verification source e.g. *Encyclopaedia Britannica volume? page ??*.

Programmes such as *Who Wants to be a Millionaire?* have, literally, a million pounds on offer. Naturally, contestants are desperate to win and even in less high-profile competitions, the stakes are high. It is not just the ignominy of losing; no-one wants to appear a fool. Nowadays, several programmes are recorded back-to-back in the same afternoon in front of a studio audience with other contestants waiting their turn in the green room. The production team, in the control room, are concentrating on getting the best pictures and the most exciting programme; they do not want and haven't time for a semantic discussion as to whether or not an answer is correct.

Accuracy of both the phrasing of the question and confirmation of the correct answer are crucial and the yea or nay is a split-second decision. 'I think so' isn't good enough.

In *Who Wants to be a Millionaire?* a valuable prize was awarded to a contestant who gave the incorrect answer. This is marginally less offensive to the audience than invalidating a correct answer so that the contestant loses when they should have won. The tabloids love it, the programme is discredited and the taint of scandal affects not only the audience rating but the programme's continuance.

## Product placement

The impartiality of programmes where one product cannot be endorsed over another is an integral part of UK broadcast regulations. Effectively, products cannot be 'plugged'.

On holiday programmes, for instance, sample holidays from different firms are featured and the names of other companies offering the same type of holiday are displayed on screen. The audience should therefore understand that there are alternatives to those being shown. Programmes cater for all purses and, depending on the programme brief, cheap holidays should be included as well as the more exotic.

The ITC insists that a variety of brands are seen, if only one is featured it could be construed as endorsement. Granada was substantially fined by the ITC when *This Morning* transmitted strands featuring only one cosmetic company's products. It is easy to speculate what happened. Daytime TV programmes have minimal budgets and certain sections of the programme (often the strands) are contracted out to independent production houses employing inexperienced (and cheap) production staff. The production team may have been offered cosmetic samples (free or at a discount) and, due to inexperience, were unaware this flouted the regulations. Mere conjecture on my part, but all too plausible.

The BBC believe their guidelines are stricter than those of the ITC (Chapter 24: Commercial Relationships and Appropriate Programme Funding 5. ITC Regulation). Does this imply commercial television programme makers can interpret the codes a little more imaginatively? When in doubt, refer to the ITC guidelines (published on the Web) or phone them for clarification.

## SPONSORSHIP

*Coronation Street* is sponsored by Cadbury's chocolate. The Barbados Tourist Board sponsors the weather on Classic FM. Sportswear firms sponsor football clubs. Sponsorship is a means whereby a commercial company identifies and aligns its 'brand image' with another product; in this case, a media programme. In return for a payment, the sponsorship company receives a specified number of seconds at the beginning and end of a programme and during the commercial breaks. The time limit is set by the ITC and cannot be exceeded.

Under no circumstances, however, can the sponsorship company influence editorial policy or programme content. At a basic level, *Coronation Street* characters won't be seen eating Cadbury's chocolate.

This is not a debate on the sponsorship issue but merely an explanation of the difference between sponsorship and product endorsement.

The BBC charter does not permit advertising or sponsored programming for any service funded by the licence fee (*BBC Producers' Guidelines*; Chapter 24: Commercial Relationships and Appropriate Programme Funding: 4 Advertising and Sponsorship).

## PROPS

Although obtaining props is the brief of the props buyer and the props department, there are times when the researcher gets involved. I once had to find a six-inch replica of Nelson (as in Nelson's Column in London). This eventually involved commissioning a sculptor to make a plaster cast mould which was turned into six resin models by a specialist prop maker.

There is also something called, helpfully, *researcher's props* (dating from when the media industry was heavily controlled by ACTT – the former film and TV union now amalgamated with other entertainment unions to become BECTU) which consist of one or two items taken on filming and for which the researcher takes responsibility; a towel for a presenter likely to get wet or a fun gizmo to be referred to in a link. The researcher's props avoid taking a separate props man on location.

The main reason for a researcher getting involved with props is when contributors bring them to studio or on location.

## Action props and standby props

These are props used as part of the action and can be as insignificant as a toothpick or a newspaper for an actor to read or as large as a lorry driven down the road – an *action vehicle* in this case. On a large production, the props men are assigned either to action or standby props.

*Standby props* are set dressing; ornaments on a mantelpiece, food in a fridge, books on a shelf.

## Action vehicles

Researchers are not expected to organise action vehicles but it occasionally happens that the action vehicle finds them. A taxidermist who collects classic cars becomes an LE item and the researcher who suggested the story in the first place coordinates the recording.

For recording in studio, the set designer needs to be informed so that space can be allocated for the car. The researcher, as the taxidermist's main contact, will coordinate the arrival and departure of the car but may need to liaise with the props department if specialist transport is required. The car, of course, may be driven to the studio. The set designer informs the stagehands where the car is to go. The floor manager must be warned as they are responsible for health and safety.

It is helpful to have the car dimensions a) so the designer knows how much space to allocate and b) to check the car can get through the dock doors (the entrance to the studio). Studios are designed for large sets but these are constructed to be assembled and pulled apart like jigsaws. The external and internal access must be clear on recording day. There is also the question of where to keep large 'props' like this when not being recorded.

For filming on location and filming from vehicles refer to Chapter 8.

## Armourers

Somebody suggests the presenter swings a pirate's sword around on location. Great – except . . .

If weapons such as swords, rifles and guns are to be used, stringent health and safety rules must be met. For this reason, it is usual to employ an armourer who knows the current regulations, will supply safe weapons and equipment and keep strict control over them whilst filming. Names of armourers can be found in the trade directories but the props department can recommend reputable and licensed armourers used in the past. Returning to the pirate's sword – use a plastic one.

The use of *replica guns* in a public place is illegal unless the police have been informed and given their permission beforehand.

Nor is it permissible to use imitation police uniforms or police cars in public; the charge is *impersonating a police officer*. Drama production and location managers are well aware of this, and the procedure involved to film legally, but a researcher must not be beguiled into dressing up a children's presenter in a facsimile uniform and filming in the middle of Trafalgar Square. The excuse 'I didn't know' is unacceptable.

## Magicians

The director of an LE show will have had wide experience of working with magicians but for daytime magazine, cable and satellite or children's programmes, it often falls to the researcher to liaise between the guest (in this case the magician) and their personal requirements. Magicians often make their own props or have them made especially for them, but occasionally (far be it from me to divulge any magician's tricks) in order to camouflage, for instance, the sound of machinery, the conjuror will request music crescendos at the crucial point. The sound department and the director must be fully aware of such requests.

## Trampolines, gymnastics and aerial work

Children's programmes often feature dramatic and visual activities like trampolining and gymnastics in studio. Trampolines are large structures and, in a specially constructed gym, are usually set into the floor to minimise accidents. In the studio, as a health and safety issue, both the trampoline frame and the height of the studio ceiling have to be considered. The director can tussle with flare from the studio lights and the unsightly gantry shots but if there isn't enough height, there is a serious problem. Safety aspects must also be considered for gymnastics and other aerial stunts such as high-wire circus acts. Check with the company health and safety officer.

## Animals

A friend of mine once set up a maggot grand national in studio. The set designer built a two-foot racecourse identical in every way and maggots were let loose (if that's the word) to squirm their way around. Afterwards, the macho Geordie stagehands refused to touch them, resulting in a plague of bluebottles the following week. Does this contravene the recent television health and safety manifesto about ensuring animals can't escape?

Studios should have guidelines for working with animals (including maggots) both in studio and on location. The guidelines are basic common sense. It is worth noting that The Dangerous Wild Animals Act 1976 (enforced by the local authorities) requires the licensing of specific wild animals and using such animals, therefore, means getting expert advice. Animal handlers experienced in television and film work are expensive but may well save hours of angst and insurance claims.

The health and safety issues are designed to cover both animals and people (for reference, see the HSE directive *Working with Animals in Entertainment*, Entertainment sheet Number 4 which can be downloaded from the Web: www.hse.gov.uk/pubns/etis4). The sort of things to be aware of are:

- *Phobias.* I have known floor managers refuse to work on shows with spiders and snakes. Members of the audience may have the same fears. Reptiles and birds are also common phobias. The back of audience tickets for *You've Been Framed* specifies if animals are to be in studio.

- *Allergies* are common. Asthmatic attacks may be brought on by cats or birds.

- *Pregnant women* are advised not to go near certain animals. Pregnant women may be involved in the audience, as contributors or part of the crew.

- Inform people with as much notice as possible so that if they do have an allergy or a phobia, there is time to replace them. Floor managers work shifts, and someone else can swap their rota.

- Organise food, water and somewhere for the animal to be kept away from noise and strange surroundings. Rehearse the item with animals last and film them first.

- Straw or hay in the studio has to be fire retardant but this is toxic for the animals so ask the owner or handler what alternatives are practicable.

- Salmonella and e-coli bacteria can be spread by farm animals and pets so the basic hygiene rules of washing after touching animals has to be stressed. All studios should have qualified first aiders present. Any accidents or bites that do occur must be reported in the accident book.

- It is unlikely that poisonous snakes or spiders are free in studio, but the handler should be aware of antidotes and it is recommended that the relevant animal is confined in some way.

This may sound alarmist but the unexpected always happens during recording. This is what makes working in television so exciting. Animals are notoriously unreliable and, as usual, let everyone know of your intentions to minimise the chance of untoward events.

Producers and directors conveniently forget that animals (and children) do not perform to order. A parrot that dances to music at home invariably won't in the studio. The pressure on its owner, who has never been in a television studio let alone one with an audience, is immense. Make huge allowances for both of them and be extremely sympathetic to the owner. My own attitude is, by all means bring the parrot into studio on the off chance it will perform, but chances are – it won't. Most producers won't thank you for telling them this.

I once had to find a pig for a fantasy fulfilment show in which a woman named Bacon was to wash a pig. Pigs, I was warned by a farmer, are unpredictable in behaviour and I was advised against the item, especially as a pig's snout is strong enough to lift the studio audience in their seats. I found a school that kept a pig as a pet. I still pale at the struggle of getting that pig from the trailer (a licence is usually required to move a pig), through the scene dock doors and onto the studio floor – a procedure made worse by the pig coming on heat that morning, leaving the props men and the pig's handler to deal with a randy sow.

## Insurance

Insurance is often overlooked. It is only recently that the media industry finally decided to give the producer overall responsibility for health and safety. Up to this point, no-one claimed responsibility and put the burden on somebody else's desk. Television companies, legally, must be insured but anything hazardous or unusual should be checked with the underwriter or broker so that, should anything go wrong, the underwriters will pay. Large television companies like Granada get their cover from several companies depending on the issues involved.

However, insurance issues are often overlooked because of ignorance.

Does the props' owner or animal handler have adequate insurance? Is it valid when they are away from home? Check what cover they have; the programme's insurance company may want details. Extra insurance cover is cheaper than claims.

In certain cases, the insurance company may request the services of a security man to ensure irreplaceable or expensive props are protected: a valuable dog collar collection, a ten-thousand pound cash prize, a celebrity guest wearing a priceless tiara. Make a special feature of it on camera. The more mean-looking the security guard, the better the television.

It is occasionally necessary to have fire officers in the studio, for instance if pyrotechnics (including lit candles) are involved. The health and safety officer can advise on this.

Whenever there is a studio audience, it is a legal health and safety require-ment to have security personnel trained in both fire and first aid, and many studio security personnel are ex-firefighters. However, if there is not an audi-ence, this may be overlooked. Should a fire-eater be taking part in a pro-gramme, it makes sense to warn the floor manager and the insurance underwriter and to have a fire officer present when the item is being recorded. The researcher must also warn the set designer who will in turn check the lighting rig (where the studio lights are situated). A sensible question for the researcher to ask is, how high do the flames go? Researchers learn the tricks of many strange trades . . .

## Risk assessment

The key to minimising the hazard during dangerous activities is, of course, risk assessment and the larger television companies are far more aware of this than they were. The BBC's risk assessment CD Rom is infamous – all BBC produc-tion staff are required to pass it and undergo risk assessment training as part of their induction. Many companies now insist that risk assessment forms are completed prior to filming or recording. More details are in Chapter 8.

Working in the media is exciting and innovative, and there are plenty of activities and situations not covered in this book. It is these that make the job so enjoyable, but original and unusual ideas have plenty of potential for going wrong. Use your professional experience and judgement and get advice from people who have been in the situation before. The more information you have, the better your background research, the less likely there are to be bud-getary or physical calamities.

*You cannot be too careful when insurance and health and safety is concerned.*

## ORGANISATION

Health and Safety Executive, Health and Safety Enquiries, Broad Lane, Sheffield, S3 7HQ
HSE, Infoline Tel 0541 545500, www.hse.gov.uk.

# 7
# Music and music programmes

The addition of music, whether it is on radio or television, makes a sequence more exciting by adding mood, atmosphere and pace. However, it can be a luxury product; why should a ninety-piece orchestra come cheap?

*All* researchers deal with music at some level at some time in their career whether it is a pop star chatting informally, performing, or both, on *Des O'Connor* or finding atmospheric music to cover a short sequence on *This Morning*. These are the most common occasions where the researcher deals with music and both concern copyright implications as well as more practical issues.

It goes without saying that a specialist music researcher is interested in music but it isn't enough to be fanatic about today's popular music; there are thousands if not millions of people with the same interest and after your job. You need an encyclopaedic passion for the history of pop, today's, yesterday's and tomorrow's, embracing the whole gamut of the industry. You will devour the music press, make friends with the record companies, especially the A & R, and attend gigs and concerts as often as a busy television schedule will allow.

On a specialist programme like *Top of the Pops* or *The Pepsi Chart Show*, enough experts are around for the researcher to gain experience from their knowledge. However, the researcher may take a more administrative role without having had experience of copyright clearance and checking music agreements. On this type of show there is little *creative* input for the researcher as the content is determined by what is in the current charts.

The perk of working on music programmes (and in television and radio in general) is that you are sent free CDs and tickets to concerts.

## CHOOSING MUSIC FOR SEQUENCES

One of the more enjoyable – and frustrating – jobs is choosing music to liven up an otherwise lacklustre sequence and enhance its atmosphere.

The only way to ensure that the music fits the topic, the mood and the style of the editing is trial and error and by playing the music alongside the relevant pictures. This involves selecting a number of tracks, all of which have been tasted beforehand either at home or the in-house music library and taking the shortlist into the edit suite. It is a lengthy process.

You will know by the *tingle factor* if the track works, even though the sequence needs trimming and tweaking for the cuts to fit the music. In other words, if the hairs on the back of your neck stand up, that's the right one.

The producer, editor and director will have suggestions of their own, in which case the researcher becomes the gopher, ordering up copies of the proposed music and, with the aid of the music department, making more selections.

## In-house music department or music library

If a radio or television station has an in-house music department, programme makers can draw on their expertise. The library staff are helpful in several ways. First, they are experts on a wide range of music and are constantly asked to help with music requests, which, together with running the music library, is their role. Like a bookshop, they order up albums and CDs (chargeable to the programme budget) and lend out music from their enormous stock. There may be an internal charge for this. Music librarians are experts on copyright issues and the royalty costs of using music and should you have a burning desire to use a piece of music which will create clearance complications or cost a huge amount, the music department will forewarn you.

The amount of royalties payable to use music is variable and what you can and can't use depends on the music agreements or the programme budget.

## Library music

The cheapest music of all is library music; music specifically composed for the media industry and intended for inclusion in audio and audio–visual productions. Each 'tune' is written to set lengths: two to three minutes, fifty-nine second versions, thirty-second versions and 5–10 second stings. Library music rarely has lyrics. Every track has a short description that tends to be a little wide of what you expect when you listen to it. Nowadays library music is recorded on CDs whereas previously they were on vinyl. Each music library has, literally, hundreds of CDs to choose from and thousands of tracks with a bewildering array of choice, making the prospect of finding a track that works with the pictures exasperatingly time consuming.

In the broadcast television and radio industry, there is considerable snobbery and disdain for library music and, in order to counteract this, the libraries go out of their way to help you pick their music instead of commercial material. With such a huge array of choice, music libraries employ consultants to help you find the appropriate track. Phone the library, describe the sequence for which you are seeking music – for example, 'I want something with a science fiction feel to cover shots of the production line at a biscuit factory' – and the consultant will suggest a suitable selection. As the library makes its profits from the royalties, the suggested CDs are sent to you free.

The alternative is to listen to the music on-line. For those companies who subscribe, the researcher can listen to the music and then have it sent down an ISDN line in real time. This is the MARS system (Multi Media Archive Retrieval System), of broadcast quality and many of the bigger music libraries subscribe to it. Zomba Production Music, for instance, currently has half its library on the system. However, at the moment, most music libraries find that people prefer the personal touch and discuss their requirements over the phone rather than deal with the Internet.

The most well-known music libraries are:

- Bruton (owned by Zomba Production Music);
- Carlin;
- Chappell (owned by Zomba Production Music);
- De Wolfe;
- KPM.

Their addresses and phone numbers, together with other music libraries, can be obtained from the Mechanical Copyright Protection Society (MCPS – see p. 105) and are listed in *The Knowledge*.

## Recorded commercial music (CDs, records, etc.)

Commercial music is dearer than library material. It has the advantage of being instantly recognisable – what *is* that tune? For well-known classical pieces there is no alternative to 'the real thing'. For lyrics appropriate to your sequence, you will also have to use commercial tracks.

The wider the transmission area, the more expensive the royalties. The cheapest is for a single transmission in the UK and the most expensive is world rights in perpetuity.

Because of the symbiotic relationship between music and radio (they cannot exist without each other) there are few potential problems in the use of commercial music for *radio* (see p. 139 and also refer to Chapter 10).

For television, however, the use of music can be problematic and mistakes are extremely costly. If a production team checks first and discovers the music they want will cost £20,000, they will go about it a different – and cheaper – way. Afterwards is too late; it's another £20,000 on the budget.

There isn't space in this book to comprehensively explain the issues but the aim is to point you in the right direction so at least you know where to go for help.

## CONDITIONS ON THE USE OF RECORDED COMMERCIAL MUSIC IN TELEVISION

A true anecdote, no names no places. . . . I once worked on a film where the director arrived with a copy of Bill Withers' *Lovely Day* to be edited over a sequence of a train speeding across the US Mid-West plains at dawn. The music worked so well that hairs stood up the back of everyone's neck, *the tingle factor* at work. The film was cut, the master print ordered and then we received notification that we couldn't use the American song and it was recut with a UK artist singing a cover version.

This story is not unusual. There are several reasons why tracks cannot be used, for example:

- the cost of world rights and especially for artists from the United States;

- the issue of *moral rights*, in other words creative work must be treated with integrity.

Some composers, publishers and copyright holders *must* be contacted beforehand for express permission to use their music as they have asserted their moral rights. They will want to know where and how the music will be used. Music departments are usually aware of who they are but for those without access to a music department, this is another reason for prior checking with the relevant agencies. Some groups never give permission. There may be any number of reasons why they turn the request down. They simply might not like how it will be used. For instance, a vegetarian band might refuse a request to play their music on an advert promoting lamb.

Irving Berlin (*White Christmas, There's No Business Like Show Business, Anything You Can Do, God Bless America* inter alia) stipulated that his music must never be parodied and his estate strictly monitors this.

*Cutting music.* When editing the film, editors often want to cut the music to fit the pictures, edit out bars or repeat choruses. This is done all the time, although editing music in this way is officially not permissible without prior consent from the copyright holders.

*Film scores.* Unless there is a 'combined use fee' or some form of buy-out clause included in the original agreement, it may not be possible to use music tracks extracted from a video or film. If you intend to do this (and they may not be broadcast quality) refer in the first instance to the Musicians Union (MU). There may be a 'combined use fee' included in the original agreement or a buy-out clause, but if there isn't, a fee will be required. The amount depends on the commercial benefit to the television company. If the score has been released on CD, follow the procedure for commercially-recorded music.

*Signature tunes.* The use of signature tunes within other programmes needs consent from the copyright holders and it may be wise to contact the MU. The *Mastermind* theme tune came from a music library and therefore is an exception to this.

*Extracts.* It used to be the case that using several solo instrument bars from a full orchestral work meant the whole orchestra had to be paid. Nowadays, this is covered in the *extract rate* in the MU/PACT agreement.

*Always* check beforehand if you can use the music the way you want to.

## COPYRIGHT

As in all creative products, someone owns the rights, and using music on a television or radio programme whether live or recorded, has to be paid for somewhere. Apart from the agreements themselves, another reason why music is such a complicated issue is because different agencies are responsible for collecting the royalties.

The main agencies are:

- the Musicians Union (MU) – acting on behalf of musicians;

- the Performing Rights Society (PRS) – acting on behalf of songwriters, composers and publishers for the public performance of broadcast copyright music in shops, concert venues and broadcasting. Collects and distributes royalties on their behalf;

- Mechanical Copyright Protection Society (MCPS) – acts on behalf of copyright holders, publishers and composers. Collects and distributes royalties. The MCPS currently has over 13,000 members, including over 9,000 writer/composer members and 4,000 publishers. Their database includes details of over three million recordings and musical works. Works in conjunction with the PRS;

- British Phonographic Industry (BPI) – the association of the UK record companies.

There are other agencies to be aware of: Equity (the actors' union), PPL (Phonographic Performance Ltd), VPL (Video Performance Ltd), ISM (Incorporated Society of Musicians), PAMRA (Performing Arts Media Rights Association) and BACS (British Academy of Composers and Songwriters) but you are most likely to encounter Equity and PPL.

## MCPS and PRS

In television and radio shows regardless of whether the music is live or recorded, both the Performing Rights Society (PRS) and the Mechanical Copyright Protection Society (MCPS) are involved.

All television and radio stations hold a PRS licence. The PRS licence, which works on a blanket principle, covers radio stations playing records and CDs live where the music is not being re-recorded. The PRS blanket licence permits the licence holder to play over 15 million musical works from jingles to symphonies. For radio stations this effectively means they can usually play whatever they like and the cost is not an issue. The tracks played are detailed on the 'P as Bs' form (Programme as Broadcast) or cue sheets and the royalties are distributed by the PRS.

The Copyright Designs and Patents Act 1988 covers the *copying* of music for use in TV and radio programmes, feature films, TV and radio commercials, videos (retail, corporate and educational), retail multi-media (computer games for instance) and products such as a free CD with a children's comic. For the use of the rights to copy, a royalty fee is normally paid.

Typical situations for this are when a band is pre-recorded to be broadcast later in the week or a CD music track is recorded (dubbed) over a documentary sequence. This is when the MCPS negotiates agreements via a licence and then redistributes the royalties to the copyright owners.

*Who owns music copyright?* This can be a variety of people – the publisher and the composer(s) for instance – but other people are also paid for the reproduction of their work: the artist performing a cover version of a song written by someone else, the musicians performing the backing track, the arranger, and the copyright holder, who may be none of these.

For CDs, minidisks and records, the place to look for the copyright information is on the sleeve, jacket or CD cover. It may be on the insert, printed on the CD itself or on the label on the vinyl disk. The information is often hard to spot.

## Music clearance

Music clearance is the term used for sorting out the payment paperwork and/or the licences.

At the BBC and the major ITV companies, the clearance usually falls to the production assistant and in radio, the broadcast assistant, researcher or producer. The MCPS blanket agreement means that usually all that needs to be completed once the programme has been made or broadcast is the 'P as Bs' form or cue sheets. For programmes with PAs or BAs, they are responsible.

However, as the researcher has been instrumental in choosing the music, they need to pass on the relevant information. The last thing a PA wants to do is chase up a freelance researcher and ask for details long since forgotten.

Because it is in everyone's interest, the MCPS and PRS have made the clearing process as simple as possible.

The MCPS needs:

- name of production;

- production type (e.g. TV broadcast, radio advertising);

- transmission area (e.g. UK, Europe, Europe and the USA, worldwide);

- number of transmissions;

- record/CD/minidisk number;

- track number;

- the title of track;

- publisher;

- composer or arranger;

- copyright owner;

- duration (this will be timed from the viewing copy).

The researcher should keep notes of the last seven bullet points.

If an independent production company is making the programme for Channel 4 or Channel 5, the music must be approved beforehand by the MCPS. The MCPS are extremely approachable.

Once the MCPS have received the form, an invoice will be sent to the production company and, on payment, the invoice becomes the licence.

## ROYALTIES

It is interesting to see the amount charged for the use of music. The MCPS rates are reviewed annually and take effect from 1 September. The examples listed are for 2000/2001.

## Commercial music

Fees are negotiated on an individual basis but the following is the MCPS suggested guidelines (June 2000):

- Channel 4           £85 per 30 seconds for 5 years (2 transmissions)
- Channel 5           £60          ,,              ,,              ,,
- SC4                 £35          ,,              ,,              ,,
- Cable and satellite £50          ,,              ,,              ,,
- Worldwide           £600–£800 per 30 seconds for 5 years (unlimited).

This does not cover advertisements, the fees for which are entirely negotiable.

## Using foreign music

You are working on a documentary about Greece and suggest adding national music for local colour. On your last holiday you picked up some Greek CDs. Can you use them?

The answer is probably yes but as always, the copyright needs to be cleared. Because the music is Greek, it is unlikely that the MCPS will have licensed it and it might be virtually impossible to find the publisher and copyright holder, especially if you don't speak Greek. The MCPS has equivalents all over the world and there will be reciprocal agreements so, by phoning the MCPS in London, you will be given a Greek contact who may even sort it all out for you. Whether or not you can afford the royalties depends on the programme budget.

For music from other countries, go through the same procedure. If there is an in-house music department, it is suggested that you contact them prior to proceeding down the MCPS route as they may feel you are usurping their professional status.

The MCPS does not cover the rights of the musicians, although they should be able to point you in the right direction. If not, speak to the MU or involve your music department.

## The MU

Most musicians earn less than £5,000 per year in an insecure, volatile profession. The MU works to improve their working conditions. In the past, the MU had a reputation for having a 'No can do' attitude, but has reversed this image into 'Can do' resulting in more work for their members.

The MU/PACT agreement defines all contingencies where musicians are involved from rehearsals, recording sessions and rates of pay. It is an all-embracing document and was revised in October 2000. It includes, inter alia:

- the cost of musicians in and out of vision in LE and other programmes;

- miming;

- live performances;

- backing tracks (see p. 103);

- the use of extracts from recordings;

- compilations.

All clearance with the MU tends to be conducted by correspondence, although there are some pro-forma forms at the back of their agreements.

Any complicated MU and other music dealings should be negotiated by the producer and the music or legal departments.

*Non-MU members.* Some stations (mainly cable and satellite) do not have an MU agreement. If this is the case, having musicians and performers in studio is controversial. Best practice says 'don't' but production companies circumvent this by using non-MU musicians. It is not uncommon for MU members to pretend not to be in the union in order to get the media exposure. Whether or not they are in the MU, it is common in these situations to perform for free. Understandably, the MU is unhappy about this and is currently under negotiation with cable and satellite companies.

## RECORDING BANDS IN STUDIO

Having a band in studio is exciting, especially if they are playing live, but it involves a lot of organisation. There are egos and costumes and instruments and all the paraphernalia of a performance combined with the pervasive hangers-on who appear to have no apparent purpose but getting in the way.

The researcher currently working on *Top of the Pops* is responsible for ensuring the Digital Audio Tapes (DATs) arrive in time from the record company as well as the bands' lyrics (these are typed into the script), assigning the dressing rooms (often the PA's responsibility), liaising between the record companies (usually the A & R department), listing the band members and their instruments together with the people accompanying them, issuing call times for the groups and writing the links for the presenter. Because there are so many groups in each programme, this is a full-time job.

On programmes such as a Saturday morning children's show where a music item could consist of the current chart topper doubling as a celebrity guest, the researcher may well work on the normal show items as well as coordinating the band's contribution.

The following is a checklist of what the researcher needs to be aware of or find:

- how many are in the group;
- the names of the group members;
- who plays which instruments;
- the band's line-up and where they stand/sit/perform;
- if they are intending to mime, sing live vocals or perform entirely live;
- if they are singing live vocals or miming, a backing track DAT will be required;
- the lyrics of the songs and, in a group, who sings what;
- a list of the equipment they are bringing;
- names of the roadies setting up the equipment and anyone else coming along with them (e.g. the A & R representative or their manager).

In return, the band must know:

- when and where they are arriving;
- where to park their vehicles;
- what time they are free to go (they may be on tour and squeezing the TV or radio programme into a busy schedule);
- what time they are recording and in what order (handing out a running order when they arrive should suffice).

If the band is from America (or anywhere outside the UK) there may be discrepancies between their equipment and the UK electrical supply and transformers and suitable power supply systems should be ordered. It is not unknown for a band's equipment to be in a dangerous condition and time should be allocated to check this before a sound check or recording takes place.

For a programme like *Top of the Pops*, where several bands perform in a single programme, each is given an area in which to perform where their roadies set up the equipment. The stage manager devises the stage plan at *Top of the Pops* but elsewhere the floor manager or even the set designer may be responsible for it. Because the researcher is the first point of contact for the record company, it often falls to them to provide the details by which the stage plan is drawn up.

On larger productions, getting the bands into wardrobe and makeup is usually the job of the floor assistant or runner working on the show. On other occasions, the researcher ensures that, after the sound check, artistes are taken to wardrobe and makeup. Women take more time in makeup than men and may want their hair washed and dressed as well. Because of this, makeup assistants prefer to start with female artistes.

A recording schedule may bear no relation to the actual running order as most shows are edited into the transmission reel. It is also common on programmes like *Top of the Pops* to record more bands than there is room for in the programme. The reason? A band may hit the Top 20 next week but is unavailable to appear because of touring commitments.

## Live music and miming

It is commonly assumed that all acts performing on programmes like *Top of the Pops* are mimed. At *Top of the Pops* this is less true than in the past as many bands enjoy performing live on television and the result is televisually more exciting. Other groups perform live vocals to a pre-recorded backing track and others, usually with an energetic dance routine, might mime the vocals whilst dancing.

*Sound checks* are performed only for bands performing live. These balance sound levels and ensure equipment is working properly. The studio sound department work with the roadies for the sound check.

Where only vocal tracks are live or the performance is entirely mimed the sound check is usually dispensed with. However, a backing track with or without vocals is required and the acquisition of this is usually the researcher's remit.

*The backing track* is relayed into studio so that everyone can hear it. The musicians play alongside and 'record to play back'. The instruments are often left unplugged and it is common practice to use a dummy drum kit. The backing track is transmitted alongside the pictures recorded in studio.

Until 1996, the MU insisted all backing tracks were re-recorded anew ensuring the musicians were paid again but this led to various dubious and questionable practices. For instance, a two-hour re-recording session was set up but, as the original track took considerably longer to record, the quality was often so poor that the track was swapped with an original. The MU frowned on this practice and occasionally sent representatives to check that the recording actually took place (it often didn't, even though the musicians were still paid) and that the tracks weren't swapped. Re-recording no longer takes place and the BPI record agreement usually contains a clause allowing the backing track to be used for miming purposes on TV and live PA systems.

Backing tracks for use in studio must be the correct format for the system. DAT is the most common.

Once the backing tracks have arrived in the production office, they need to be sent to the sound department. It is common courtesy to return them as soon as possible if the companies want them back.

## Pop videos

Pop videos are the mainstay of many programmes simply because they are very much cheaper than performance. Nowadays, the agreement for broadcasting pop videos without incurring extra payments to the musicians or band is contracted when the videos are made.

## Sessions players

Sessions players are freelance musicians earning a living by playing an instrument at a recording session. A sessions musician renowned for, say, his saxophone playing will not relish the prospect of someone appearing in studio playing his solo. Unfortunately, a record company may not regard the brilliant but bald saxophonist as fitting the image for a girl band and decide to replace him with someone more attractive.

This is permissible only within the MU/PACT agreement if the original musician consents to the substitution. The record company should organise the swap but it is in the interests of the TV company that the researcher double-checks consent has been obtained. In the first instance, speak to the A & R representative.

What does the researcher do during the recording day? Crisis management mainly. The beginning of the day is frantic with writing links (if not done previously), ensuring the presenter and everyone else knows what is going on as well as fielding the phone and dealing with various problems as the bands make their way to the studios. Once the rehearsals and recording are under way, the researcher's job is to troubleshoot and check that everybody knows what is happening and where they should be. If the job has been done properly beforehand and no untoward events occur (acts of war and God that nobody can predict or anticipate) the researcher may hover between studio, control room and production office for referral in case of queries and problems.

## ORGANISATIONS

*The Knowledge;* Miller Freeman PLC, Riverbank House, Angel Lane, Tonbridge, Kent TN9 1SE, Tel 01732 362666, www.theknowledgeonline.com.

MU, 60–62 Clapham Road, London SW9 0JJ, Tel 020 7582 5566, www.musiciansunion.org.uk.

*Music Weekly Yearbook.*

MCPS, 29–33 Berners Street, London W1P 4AA, Tel 020 7580 5544, www.mcps.co.uk.

PACT, 45 Mortimer Street, London W1N 7TD, Tel 020 7331 6700, www.pact.co.uk.

PRS, 29–33 Berners Street, London W1P 4AA, Tel 020 7580 5544, www.prs.co.uk.

*The White Book*: Bank House, 23 Warwick Road, Coventry, CV1 2EW, Tel 024 7655 9658, www.whitebook.co.uk.

VPL, Video Performance Ltd, 1 Upper St James Street, London W1R 3HG, Tel 020 7534 1400.

# 8
# Filming on location

Once a researcher has set up filming, they usually go on location with the crew. They are responsible for ensuring everything goes well, acting in a variety of roles from gopher through to ensuring that anyone they brought on location knows what is happening and feels well cared for. They may pay expenses to contributors and ensure they sign the release (permission) forms although both of these responsibilities will be carried out by the PA if there is one on the crew. With a small crew, the researcher minds any props and special requirements such as towels and clothing. Organising the location and equipment involved is part of the pre-production schedule.

A small production hasn't the budget for a location or production manager and therefore the researcher, together with the PA, may book hotels, transport and any other administrational details. They may even organise the shooting schedule which, for a drama, is the role of the first assistant director (shortened to 1st AD; the floor manager does this in studio) but the producer may prefer to organise it him or herself.

Before anyone goes on location, a *recce* should be carried out. This can be combined to meet possible contributors and in this case you must ask yourself – do I want to include them as a contributor? Is their story relevant and good enough?

## THE RECCE – RECONNAISSANCE

One of my most memorable experiences in television was a day spent with the RAF in Yorkshire setting up an item on fast jet pilot training. It revealed all sorts of situations. The time it took to measure me up (and therefore the crew) for the ejector seat. Would the cameraman fit? Would the camera? If the camera dimensions were too big I needed to order another that would fit. Could the cameraman and director fly in the same plane? No, so how many planes could be supplied for filming? Did the crew require special clothing?

Would the RAF kit them out? Did they need the cameraman's measurements? Which ones? Could we film on the runway? Where was I to obtain earmuffs and to what specification?

This particular assignment also drew to my attention the little detail of dress in the officers' mess. If we were to lunch there, the men had to wear jacket and tie, not jeans. For women (the PA and myself), it was 'smart casual' but not trousers. Plenty more issues were raised during the day and filming would have been pretty stressful without such a detailed recce. The organisation on the RAF's part was, as usual, supremely professional.

Effectively, a recce should tell you everything, including:

- Is the location suitable?

- What special equipment is required to film there?

- Are there any sound or camera problems?

- What risks are taken to film there?

And:

- how to get there and how long it takes;

- how easy it is to find the location;

- where to go for lunch.

Napoleon said that an army marches on its stomach but he hadn't met a film crew.

Let us now look at the *essential* points to consider on a recce.

## 1   CONTACTS

- Who are you meeting? Their name, designation, address, phone number. Is there a direct line or must you go through the switchboard?

- Whenever possible, get the direct line number even if it's ex-directory. It's extremely time wasting to go through an automated system before speaking to the person you want, especially on location.

- What story do they have to tell, if any? How articulate are they? Is their story coaxed out of them or are they natural talkers? Their appearance shouldn't be an issue but is (refer to Chapter 4) unless it's for radio.

- Can they grant filming permission or must they refer up? How long will this take?

## 2   EVENTS

- What happens? Recce the event at the same time it is scheduled to take place. In other words, if you are filming on a Wednesday, schedule the recce for a Wednesday. This reveals snags like Concord flying overhead when you are expecting to film – i.e. sound problems.

- If possible, see the event first. If it is a one-off, it is essential to see the location before you film.

- How many people are there? How many take part? How many watch? What do they wear? How noisy are they?

Whilst you are filming, the crew and director (if it isn't you) will keep asking what happens next and where is the best place to film from? You need to know everything.

## 3   DIRECTIONS

- How do you get there? I was once given instructions to go to the second house on the right after the public phone box. Seven miles down the road and five cattle grids later, I found the phone box. The second house on the right was a mile and a half further. Maps are helpful, verbal instructions are (usually) better.

- Directions need to be relayed to the crew. Write them down as soon as you can, for instance when you arrive at your destination.

- On large drama shoots, it is common for the production manager to erect signs on the road indicating the correct direction and ensuring no-one gets lost and no-one over-claims travel expenses.

## 4   PRINTED LITERATURE, PRE-PUBLICITY, MAPS

- Pick up all printed literature publicising the event and anything else which may be helpful.

- If there are maps of the hospital, shopping centre, factory, government building, etc., collect them, too.

## 5   PARKING

- Where does the crew park? Do they need money for meters or 'pay and display'? Can special parking be arranged? The police and local authorities cannot usually arrange parking spaces for filming but for large drama shoots they will be as helpful as they can.

- The parking for the crew must be as secure as possible and as physically near to where filming takes place. There is a lot of expensive and heavy kit to carry.

## 6    EASE OF ACCESS – CONSIDER THE FOLLOWING

- Is it easy to get to and easy to film in?

- Does someone have to find a key to let you in?

- Are there places the film crew cannot go? Golf clubs in particular forbid women in certain rooms. There may be females on the crew.

- Are there a lot of stairs to climb? Is there a lift? Is it in the middle of nowhere and how far from the road? Are there steep slopes? Near water?

- *Security passes.* Will you need security passes? If you are filming on Ministry of Defence land, government property or somewhere equally politically sensitive, it is common for the crews' names to be faxed a few days beforehand for security clearance. Under these circumstances, security passes are occasionally pre-issued and sent to the office to be handed out to the crew before they film.

- Check if any other information such as full names, date and place of birth and photographs are required for security checks.

## 7    LIGHTING

- Will a basic lighting kit (two redheads and a blonde plus sungun, gels and filters) be enough or do you need more? For a large area, the film crew or film office need to be informed beforehand.

## 8    POWER SUPPLIES

- How far is the nearest electricity supply? Must you order extra cables? Is there an electricity supply or do you need a genny (generator)? This is only necessary in very large shoots or OBs and it is unlikely you would be doing the recce on your own. In very large establishments, especially factories, you need to check the voltage in case an adapter is required. This is even more important if you are filming abroad where 240 volts is not standard.

Because of health and safety requirements, some television companies insist on sending extra 'sparks' (nickname for an electrician), particularly when filming in schools and hospitals. They stand by the lights ensuring nobody accidentally walks into them. Also, should there be a mains disconnection, there will be at least two people to work on the reconnection.

## 9    NOISE

- Schools, hospitals, factories and airports are very noisy. Muzak in shopping centres is a hindrance to filming and will need copyright clearance.

- If the location is really noisy, an airport or factory, earmuffs might be obligatory.

Most sound recordists insist that ambient noise (especially muzak and background hum of machinery) is turned off whenever possible. They are excellent at locating both the source and people responsible for turning it off. Some noisy machinery, life-saving medical equipment for instance, cannot be turned off.

Filming directly under a flight path creates difficulties for the editor who cannot cut from a noisy 'plane overhead' shot to a quiet shot without it being pretty obvious. If a plane flies overhead, the take is usually reshot. The same applies in a shopping arcade where one shot in a sequence has 'Blue Suede Shoes' in the background and the next 'Yesterday'.

Under such circumstances, either find a quieter location or warn the director/sound recordist beforehand and be prepared for a long day's shoot with plenty of retakes.

## 10    CATERING

- Where is the nearest suitable restaurant? How long does it take to drive from the location? What time does it open/shut? Can you pre-book? How expensive is it? (There is usually a budget limit.) Is there a variety of meals to cater for vegetarians? How secure is the car parking?

On large drama shoots, a location catering company may be contracted to feed crew and actors. The responsibility for booking them falls to the location manager.

## 11    TOILETS

- If filming at someone's house or an office block, this is not a problem. It is a concern in the middle of nowhere, but less so for men who can utilise the nearest bush.

- If filming in a shopping centre, check where the nearest public lavatories are.

My advice is to use the loo whenever you see one even if you don't want it at the time.

## HEALTH AND SAFETY WHEN GOING UNACCOMPANIED ON A RECCE

There are several basic precautions to take when you make an unaccompanied recce and are effectively the same as meeting a programme contributor (Chapter 4).

* Tell someone where you are going and when you are due back.

* If you are meeting someone for the first time, meet in a public place if possible.

* Take a mobile phone with you, leave it switched on but don't use it while driving.

* Park in a well-lit area.

* Ensure you have enough petrol in the car.

## RISK ASSESSMENT

It is common practice nowadays to complete a risk assessment form after a recce and before filming and in some cases the shoot will not be sanctioned until the form has been signed by various line managers, including the producer.

The HSE publish a useful checklist covering and expanding on risk assessment.

## RECCE NOTES

On your return to the office, write down all your impressions, together with phone numbers and contacts.

If you didn't like the location but the people were good, why not consider importing them somewhere else. You will have to consider the ethical and political implications. There is a diplomatic problem with liking the location but not the people, especially if they are integral to the location. Under these circumstances, the judicious way is to start again with a new set of people at a different location.

## FINDING LOCATIONS

This is easy when interviewing someone in their home, office, or a hospital. You can probably film there. The considerations of filming in public places are discussed later. However, there are times when the location is not immediately obvious and you need to find somewhere suitable.

The immediate and easiest answer is to ask the person you are filming if they can suggest somewhere. Get them to describe it fully before accompanying them on the recce. If, when you get there, the location isn't suitable or you can't get filming permission, find somewhere else. Your contributor may be able to help. If they say unhelpfully, 'This is where I always go', either change the contributor, or find somewhere else and tactfully persuade them to be filmed there instead.

Finding somewhere from scratch involves ingenuity. Colleagues, especially production and location managers, may make helpful suggestions. The local film or tourist office can help. The governing association is worth a try as are clubs or other people involved in the same pursuit. Follow up all suggestions and recce each one until you find what you want or the time runs out and you must compromise.

Historical and technical accuracy is occasionally a consideration, although location filming is notorious for taking liberties. The Virginia scenes for Granada's *Moll Flanders* were shot in the West Country. Prague doubled for revolutionary Paris in *The Scarlet Pimpernel*. Who said the camera never lies?

## FACILITY FEES

If you film in locations owned by the National Trust and other such organisations, be prepared to pay a facility fee. Some locations are only too pleased at the extra publicity, merely charging a token fee to cover extra staff and electricity, but others charge on a sliding scale depending on the time you take, the type of programme and the amount of trouble you put them to. Unless it's a drama or OB – when the location manager will negotiate fees – you are unlikely to be asked an exorbitant fee.

Remember to check first. Producers take the presentation of an unexpected invoice extremely badly.

When filming in someone's home, it is common courtesy to offer a token payment for their electricity and time. This depends, of course, on the budget but £5 or £10 should suffice. Again, check with the producer.

## LOCATION FILES

In one BBC production office, individual researchers keep a location file. Whenever they encounter an interesting potential location on the way to work or in the daily papers, they note it or cut out the relevant article and stick it in the file. To a certain extent, the file is out of date pretty quickly as locations change; building sites, for instance, do not remain building sites very long. When a specific location is called for, the researchers rummage through their location files and nearly always turn up something useful.

## FILMING PERMISSION

Organising filming permission can wait until you are back in the office but is worth being aware of whilst making the recce.

If you intend to film on *private land*, permission must be obtained from the owner. Shopping precincts such as Bluewater, Lakeside, the Metro Centre and the Trafford Centre are all private properties requiring permission to film. Open-air precincts are also often private land.

The precinct manager can give permission for filming in the public areas but should you wish to film inside individual shops separate permission is required from the shop manager. They may need to refer to head office and it is common to be asked what you intend to film and why.

Merely filming shop fronts without permission can instigate awkward moments although most film crews do it, especially in the local high street. The best practice is to obtain authority to film a shop frontage before taking out a crew. Pop inside and ask the manager. For filming outside their shop fronts they usually say yes instantly. Keep a note of the person who gave permission in case they have a day off on the day concerned. Some managers are more cautious and if the shop is one of a chain, it may involve a phone call to the head office. The big companies' phone numbers are found in *The Media Guide*, and those, together with the smaller ones, are listed in a business directory such as *Kelly's* or *ASLIB*.

Ask in the first instance to be put through to the *Public Affairs Department*, *Public Relations* or *Press Office* and see how you fare. In some cases, the PR is handled by an outside agency and you may find that obtaining permission is neither straightforward nor quick with everyone enquiring about the programme, the content and how the footage will be used.

*Filming in the street* also officially requires permission. The police should be informed but if there is a local film office, they may do this for you. (Please note that film offices are not a replacement for general research and are too busy to answer questions such as 'What is the phone number for the local taxi rank?')

Take the name of the police officer granting permission. Should an officer stop you in the street, you can refer back. In busy areas (especially Central London) permission is not guaranteed and there may be stipulations such as hand-held filming only (i.e. no tripods) and moving on if the police consider you are causing an obstruction. The police have the power of arrest for causing a breach of the peace or a disturbance. This is especially relevant in Central London and other cities.

It is not unknown for film crews to record in the street without police permission. On the whole, the police ignore them unless they are causing an obstruction. This is not best practice although for news items during riots and civil unrest, the police wouldn't have given permission anyway. It is unusual for researchers to be crewmembers during civil disturbances but riots occasionally start unexpectedly and television personnel get involved simply because they are there. The presence of cameras may even be the catalyst for upheaval when filming marches and demonstrations where people do not want to be filmed. The HSE guidance has advice on this.

For large drama shoots and OBs the location or production manager will handle film permission.

## RELEASE FORMS

Release forms are signed by contributors to prove they have given their permission to be filmed and for the footage to be edited and transmitted. Often the release forms are used as a receipt for payment. The responsibility for getting release forms signed is usually taken by the PA although the researcher, who has a rapport with the contributor, may do it instead. On shoots where there is no PA, it is the researcher's responsibility to ensure the release forms have been signed.

The actual nature of the release form depends on the production company. In some, the rights of the contributor would appear to be non-existent and I have known people refuse to sign, especially if there are clauses giving the production company the right to include the footage in any programme, edited in any format and without the contributor seeing or vetting the cut footage before transmission (this is technically against the BSC guidelines). The words of one release form from one TV company alarmed contributors so much that the PAs nicknamed the form 'the blood chitty'.

Should a contributor refuse to sign a release form, legally you cannot use them in a programme even if they have already been filmed. However, if they stipulate the footage can be used in the programme for which they have been filmed but no other, then the footage can be used for just that.

Filming in a school involves the administrative headache of having parental or guardian permission for every child likely to be involved and this can mean the entire school. Children whose parents or guardians refuse (or forget) to sign cannot be filmed. The head-teacher gives authority to film in a school.

There are ethical considerations when using footage containing children. In a film about child abuse the viewer may construe that the featured children have been abused. This contravenes several codes of conduct. For guidance refer to them.

The hospital administrator or chief executive gives permission for filming in a hospital. There are also ethical issues of filming people in hospital and whose appearance

> is not incidental, where they are not random and anonymous or where, though unnamed, they are shown in particularly sensitive situations (for example as psychiatric or intensive care patients), individual consents to use this material should be sought. Any exceptions should be justifiable in the public interest.
>
> (*The ITC Programme Code:* 2 Privacy, Gathering of Information, etc., 2.2(i)
> Filming and Recording in institutions, etc.)

However, people in this situation are often too ill to sign a form and here, the next of kin can sign it. *The ITC Programme Code* states:

> When by reason of disability or infirmity a person is not in a position either to give or to withhold agreement, permission to use the material should be sought from the next of kin or from the person responsible for their care.
>
> (ibid.)

If, between recording and transmission, someone passes away, it is imperative that the next of kin are contacted for permission – tactfully sought – before the broadcast. The relatives may wish the broadcast to be cancelled in deference to the deceased.

## CALL SHEETS

On a small production (or a relatively large one on a tight schedule), you may be the only person who knows what and where you are filming.

For those who need to know, the information is communicated on a call sheet. On large productions, especially dramas, the call sheet is devised, written and updated by the 1st AD and is distributed to all crew members, actors and walk ons; in short, to everyone involved. Individual companies and production teams have their own house style but the required information is standard.

Call sheets include:

- title of production;
- date of filming;
- date of transmission (written as 'tx') if known;
- personnel and their designations, e.g. cameraman;
- crew mobile phone numbers, e.g. the director's, yours, the PA's;

- the location, address, contact names and numbers. The crew like to know who they are meeting and address them by name;

- time of filming – include whatever is relevant:
  - crew call times,
  - leaving time from base (time is needed to load equipment into the car),
  - travel time,
  - estimated arrival on location,
  - set up time,
  - rehearsal time if any,
  - filming time,
  - wrap time,
  - location departure times (time is needed to load equipment),
  - arrival back at base,
  - off clock time (after equipment has been stored away),
  - don't forget to include important times such as when an event is scheduled to start and finish. The crew sets up beforehand so that they can start shooting as soon as events get underway;

- the base address, especially if you are travelling, e.g. hotel name and phone numbers;

- transport arrangements, for example who is travelling with whom, train and plane times and numbers;

- meeting place before you leave to film – crew room, hotel lobby;

- directions – always include both maps and written instructions. Highlight the destination in red. Give distance and time estimates. Are you crossing toll bridges? Is cash required?

- car parking arrangements. Include maps if possible. Is cash required for parking?

- is there a long walk, difficult route from the car park to the location?

- meal arrangements, address and phone numbers;

- is special equipment required? Clothing? Lighting? Other equipment?

- health and safety requirements;

- brief synopsis. The crew always ask what they are filming but it is helpful to give a two- or three-line synopsis at the end of the call sheet. In a drama call sheet, this is essential.

# FILMING CONSIDERATIONS IN PUBLIC AND SENSITIVE PLACES

## Filming people in public places

If they are not central figures in the item, one doesn't need permission from everyone who 'just happens to be there at the time'. The same applies for people filmed in hospitals (see p. 115), factories and department stores. The ITC guidelines read

> it is very likely that the material will include shots of individuals who are themselves incidental, rather than central, figures in the programme. The question arises how far and in what conditions such people retain a right to refuse to allow material in which they appear to be broadcast. As a general rule, no obligation to seek agreement arises when the appearance of the persons shown is incidental and they are clearly random and anonymous members of the general public.
>
> (*The ITC Programme Code:* 2 Privacy, Gathering of Information, etc., 2.2(i) Filming and recording in institutions, etc.)

Obviously, should someone come up to you and object, the footage containing them cannot be used. Most people, on the whole, don't mind.

There are ways and means of avoiding disputes. Where members of the public gather, for instance in a pub (which is private property and filming permission should be obtained beforehand), a large notice informing customers that filming is taking place inside means that, should they enter, they are assumed to have given their consent to be filmed.

However, people may resent being filmed for a variety of reasons especially in politically or socially sensitive places. Being filmed in Manchester's gay village may be one of them, especially if viewers assume (wrongly) that everyone in Manchester's gay village *is* gay. Your risk assessment prior to filming will reflect this.

## Filming from bicycles and motor bikes

Let's get filming from bicycles out of the way first. This is the biggest no-no ever. It is both dangerous and illegal. And yes, ambitious researchers working on satellite television programmes wanting to make a 'mark for themselves' have attempted what they think will be a spectacular shot. There are serious repercussions; it will get you fired, arrested and maybe killed. Not necessarily in that order. And don't think you can sneak the shot in. Once it is transmitted, the HSE will demand to know how you got such an interesting effect – and then you will be fired.

Filming from the back of motorbikes is another taboo. Cameramen filming the London Marathon are specially trained, their bikes adapted and the cameras fitted to mounts specifically for that purpose. When directing a cameraman filming from the back of a motorbike, the researcher must be sure the cameraman is fully insured to do so, is trained and has taken the appropriate health and safety measures including the wearing of appropriate protective clothing and having the camera fixed to a camera mount.

## Filming from cars

Filming from a car is far less problematic although, again, certain measures must be taken to ensure crew and general public are in no danger of being injured.

The car must be driven according to the Highway Code and the driver must obey all legal requirements. The HSE guidelines offer general filming guidelines when filming on the roadside and from vehicles (including motorbikes) and the following sums up their points for specifically filming from a car:

- a seat belt must always be worn;

- shooting through a sun roof is too dangerous and is not allowed;

- when shooting through a side window (with seat belt on) don't lean out and don't let the camera lens protrude beyond the plane of the car;

- tracking should not be done from the boot of a saloon car or from any open doors;

- tracking from car to car should only be done on private roads unless you have police permission;

- if filming up and bys (when a car drives up to and past the camera) from the roadside, the camera and tripod must be a least a metre from the edge of the road and on the inside of any bends;

- when filming up and bys, walkie talkies should be used to communicate with the driver as to when it is safe to drive into shot. Drivers must not be expected to use walkie talkies and drive simultaneously;

- it is illegal to race on public highways.

This sums up the more obvious points but basically means that filming POV (point-of-view) shots through a car window is perfectly permissible as long as the relevant precautions mentioned above are taken. Your employer must, by law, have issued their own local guidelines and you should be knowledgeable of them before filming. If you don't comply and an accident happens, not knowing the rules will not act in your defence.

As a general rule, let the cameraperson do the difficult shots. If you are filming on your own, filming from a vehicle is unsafe unless the camera does not require an operator, is switched on before driving away and switched off after the shot is finished when the car is parked in a safe position. An example of a self-operated camera is one mounted on the front of a racing car and often referred to as a 'zap camera'. (The term dates from when they were 'zapped off', i.e. fell off more often than stayed on.) Nowadays these self-operated devices tend to be small digicams.

To film something elaborate such as five vintage cars driving down the road, it is expedient on a health and safety angle (as well as legal) to film on private land. There is more control and with the added dimension of a scenic background.

Railways and stations are other public places where you may wish to film. These can take time to set up, I mean days rather than hours unless you have already got good contacts.

The main problem with filming on railways is discovering who owns what. Since privatisation, Railtrack owns the track and stations whereas several different companies own the trains and their routes. After the Hatfield train crash in October 2000, the government is rethinking the railway system; the number of train companies and track ownership may have changed since writing this book. If you film on the rail network, expect to pay a facility fee.

The main numbers for the rail companies is found in the all-embracing *Media Guide*. At the time of writing, individual stations are no longer listed in the phone book or 192 Directory Enquiries Service.

## Railway safety

When filming on stations remember that the general public are rushing to catch trains and not looking for tripods. The crew should consist of enough people to keep both personnel and equipment safe. Don't place the camera close to the edge of the platform especially if high-speed trains go through the station; in other words, if a yellow line has been painted on the platform don't cross it to film. The voltage on the railway system is considerably more than the wiring at home and electricity can 'jump' gaps of up to 9 feet. It's common safety practice for a railway official to accompany you when you are filming. Heed their advice.

Airports are (in my experience) more helpful. It's obviously hard to get permission to film beyond customs and immigration control as these are technically 'out of the country' and, just as in a railway station, an airport official will accompany the crew at all times. Phone numbers can be found in the

Phone Book, Directory Enquiries Service (192), the *Media Guide* and many others. If you do get to film on the runway, earmuffs will be required and health and safety issues are vital.

Filming in court during a trial is impossible under the sub judice laws, which is why news programmes broadcast illustrations by court artists.

Filming in prisons and juvenile institutions is notoriously difficult and it is time-consuming to gain permission (if given at all).

The governor is the person to approach for filming permission in a prison. S/he may need to consult a higher authority and approval takes a long time. If the subject matter is trivial, expect to be turned down.

A list of all crewmembers will be required prior to setting foot on the premises. Once in, prison routine takes precedence over filming and the crew must work around it. They will be accompanied at all times and locked in and out through a succession of doors, all of which takes up valuable filming time so the film schedule will have to take account of this. The security is two way; many prisoners are dangerous and the crew's safety is paramount.

If you intend to film prisoners, prior permission from the prisoners themselves is obligatory. Because of the nature of their crimes, this is usually difficult to get. The feelings of their victims must be taken into account and you may cause offence to both the victim and the viewer.

Churches and places of worship are far simpler to set up. The vicar, priest, minister or dean is the person to approach in the first instance. However, the final authority for the Church of England lies with the Chapter of the Cathedral or the Parochial Church Council. If you are filming a service, remember that the words are covered by copyright. Also, remember that for many people, their place of worship is sacred and is to be treated with respect.

Theatres and concert halls have their own pitfalls – the people. Filming in a theatre and concert hall per se is not a problem unless you want to film actors or musicians. The Musicians Union and Equity exist to counteract the appalling employment records and level of pay for their members and there are minimum union rates for filming any of their members. This usually involves an official contract via the casting department. The theatre management will also insist that any of their staff, cleaners, electricians, security men are paid for their time. As usual for dramas, the location or production manager together with the casting department will organise everything but these points should be borne in mind should you suggest a 'quickie' shot back-stage at the local rep.

## HAZARDOUS ACTIVITIES

All activities are risky, even crossing the road if the correct precautions aren't taken, but in filming terms, some are regarded as more hazardous than others.

Filming from a helicopter requires a considerable amount of setting up, not least because of Civil Aviation rules. There have been an inordinate number of fatal accidents involving film crews and helicopters and it is officially regarded as a hazardous activity.

The quickest way of finding a company who will charter helicopters is to telephone the Civil Aviation Authority or the local airfield.

You *must* use a licensed operator (one holding a CAA Air Operator's Certificate) and preferably one with filming experience.

A reputable firm will insist on a camera mount. There are three main types: rubber vibration mounts, balance mounts and high quality gyro stabilised camera spheres. The one you choose depends on your budget and the sort of shots required. If in doubt, get the cameraman or director to contact the helicopter firm direct.

The mount usually needs to be ordered up specially. Ensure everyone knows from where it has been ordered and where it needs to be delivered or collected. It also needs to be returned on time or an excess hire charge may be incurred. The film unit office may order it for you.

There is usually little room in a helicopter (except for the larger, very expensive ones) for crewmembers other than the cameraman and director.

Hiring a helicopter is expensive. They charge by the flying hour and this includes the flying time to and from the location. Helicopter companies expect to be chartered for at least two hours. Charges are upwards of £600 per hour depending on the size of the chopper and the current cost of aviation fuel.

Helicopters are not obliged to have third party liability insurance although those with the Air Operator's Certificate are required to do so. Check with the helicopter company but also inform the production company's underwriters of the crew who will be flying. Because of the helicopter's hazardous status, both personnel and equipment need to be specifically covered.

Chartered helicopters cannot fly at night, in fog, over highly populated areas or large areas of water but the quality of the shot cannot be reproduced and, if you get the chance to fly in a helicopter, take it. It is an amazing experience and one of the perks of working in television.

For further information about filming from helicopters, the British Film Commission's *Check Book* is excellent and the health and safety official at the station will also offer guidance as well as production and location managers and the CAA.

Light aeroplanes are less versatile for filming although cheaper than helicopters. The main criteria for commissioning helicopters also applies to light aircraft and the insurance underwriters must be informed.

## Dangerous locations

What constitutes a dangerous location? Sticking a camera at the top of a cliff is obviously one but everything is relative. The hard shoulder of a motorway is lethal. Production companies are nowadays extremely conscious of health and safety issues and in most cases you will not be permitted to film without having completed a risk assessment form. Crews are excellent at taking care of themselves but tragedies still happen – usually on location. If in doubt, check with the safety officer where you are working. A change of location may be required.

When filming a particularly dangerous event, check the *insurance* cover. It is also essential to check the public liability insurance. Chapter 6 has some general insurance advice.

## Stuntmen and stunt arrangers

The producer, the location or the production manager usually hires these but it is useful to be aware of who they are and what they do. Most stunts are choreographed by stunt arrangers, often ex-stuntmen too old to perform the stunts themselves but with enough expertise and knowledge to set up stunts safely and dramatically. Until relatively recently, there were no stuntwomen and stunts for women were provided by thin men in wigs. There are still only a handful or so women in the industry. Stuntmen and arrangers tend to be specialists in pyrotechnics, cars, fight scenes and so on. The trick is the editing together of the video to make the action seamless and fluid. Action sequences, like all films, are shot in sections.

Although the general researcher is not often involved in dramas on this scale, they may well find themselves involved in a documentary about 'The Making of . . .' such and such a film. It is useful, therefore, to have an idea of the questions to ask the stunt arranger before sending out the documentary crew to film the drama crew. Television drama involves filming sequences from many different angles but, in stunt work, it is understandable if the first take is the only take. Be prepared.

A simplistic sequence might be where an out of control lorry overturns and the people inside are trapped. The stunt arranger might set it up like this. A lorry is driven down a road in the first shot. For the second shot, it goes up a ramp fitted with what is effectively a cannon. The exploding cannon (unseen by the viewer) turns the lorry over. The camera cuts and the stunt driver climbs out. Cue smoke and fire for the next shot through the broken window to a shot of dummies burning inside. Nowadays, with computer-generated graphics, the audience would see the burning actors.

It is illegal to use weapons – including replica ones – in public places. Location managers and 1st ADs are aware of this but do not be tempted to shoot a 'fun' item in a Bristol street involving a pretend gun and a children's presenter. It is also illegal to impersonate police officers so the children's presenter cannot wear a pretend police uniform. Other rules for filming in public places will be found in the British Film Commission's *Check Book* and *The Knowledge* and for further guidance on all issues mentioned in this chapter, consult the regulatory bodies' programme codes.

## PERSONAL PRACTICALITIES

### Clothing

Standing around in freezing weather during filming is tantamount to torture. And if it is raining as well . . . I knew a PA whose hair froze into icicles under a rain machine during a night shoot.

Be prepared. Forget looking attractive on a film shoot, being cold is a bigger turn off. A thick impermeable jacket with hood and removable lining is essential. Ensure it is rainproof. Five hours in the rain penetrates most clothing. Eight hours leaves you wet and numbingly cold.

Remember the anatomy below the waist. Lorry drivers often wear tights under their trousers. So do film crews. I've been known to wear two pairs of tights with two pairs of socks under thermal long johns and jeans – and still been perishingly cold.

Even with a hood, a woolly hat is recommended; most heat loss is through the head. A PA was taken to hospital with hypothermia because she didn't wear a hat.

Umbrellas are supplied for the camera and equipment. PAs often carry a spare umbrella. Researchers are advised to carry their own in the boot. If nothing else, it keeps the clipboard dry. Pencils, under such conditions, are more useful than biros.

Keep wellingtons permanently in the boot. You might need them on both recces and filming.

Summer has its own drawbacks. Shorts are great. So are t-shirts but take and use plenty of sunscreen and *always* wear a sun hat or baseball cap especially for those who are thinning on top. Drink plenty of water.

Because filming is so concentrated, it is easy to forget to slap on the suncream and to forget the water intake. This is the road to sunstroke.

Whenever you see a lavatory – use it. You never know when the next one will turn up. This is not so important for men but vital for women.

## Relationship warning

Working on location means long hours under high pressure. People get very close within an extremely short period of time and sex is often inevitable. When you get home, the frisson evaporates.

Be warned, most location relationships do not last but cause the break-up of previous relationships. No wonder marriages are notoriously short-lived in the film and television industry.

## SUMMARY

- Always leave a location tidier than when you arrived.

- Keep noise and disruption to a minimum. Respect the general public and the local residents.

- You cannot do too much preparation.

- Be aware of all health and safety aspects.

## FURTHER READING

Holland, Patricia, *The Television Handbook*, Routledge, 2nd edn, 2000.
Jarvis, Peter, *Essential Television Handbook*, Focal Press, 1996.
Maier, Robert, *Location Scouting and Management Handbook*, Focal Press, 1994.
Small, Robin, *Production Safety for Film, Television and Video*, Focal Press, 2000. This is an excellent book on health and safety covering all aspects in great detail.
Watts, Harris, *On Camera, Essential Know-how for Programme Makers*, Aavo, revised 1997. An excellent book on all aspects of programme making.

## ORGANISATIONS

Health and Safety Executive; see the Appendix.

The ITC, Radio Authority and BBC guideline details are in the Appendix.

# 9
# Filming abroad

Researchers occasionally film abroad which is a perk of the job. Most of the information in the previous chapter will be relevant but filming abroad has its own idiosyncrasies and complications, not least stomach upsets.

Filming abroad is exciting. You see new places and meet interesting people while someone else foots the bill. The downside is that you are working and are not a tourist. The rest of the crew may finish once filming is over for the day, but you are bashing a red-hot phone checking everything for tomorrow is flawless.

In a large television company or for a prestigious programme, the location or production manager will book flights, coordinate hotels, arrange internal transport and the shipment of equipment. Large companies have accounts with travel agencies and the transport details are left to them. Bear in mind, however, that you are the one sorting out problems at the sharp end and your company is employing the travel agency.

I am assuming in this chapter that you are not working under especially difficult conditions such as war or civil unrest. Obviously, there are many dangers and health and safety issues working as a foreign correspondent for a news station and other books specialise on this subject.

The following information will help you know what you are up against even if you are not personally responsible for the organisation, although for those working for cable and satellite stations it is increasingly common for a researcher to film alone abroad.

## BEFORE YOU GO

### Local customs, holidays, religious festivals and weather

Before you embark on filming abroad, check when local holidays, customs and religious festivals take place. Not all parts of the world celebrate Christmas or

Easter and countries celebrate festivals unique to themselves. The country's tourist office can offer guidance on local customs but their motivation, of course, is to attract tourists to their country and they cannot be expected to give a detrimental view of it.

Of course, these regional festivals may be the reason you are filming, but if they are not, transport arrangements, car hire and the functioning of the hotel can be cancelled, curtailed and seriously impaired with repercussions on filming and budgets.

Climate can also cause difficulties. Check if you are filming during the monsoon, hurricane season or rainy season. If you are filming during a festival or extremes of weather, expect problems.

## Logistics

It's no good intending to be in Istanbul on 3 May, if the travel agency hasn't been told. Also, logistically speaking, planes may not fly direct from Istanbul to the next location in Stockholm, making it unfeasible to shoot there two days later. The production manager and the travel agent will work alongside each other to organise the logistics but they need the information first and the production office may have to compromise. Health and safety issues (and union rules) insist that rest days are scheduled. Accidents are more likely to occur when people are exhausted and constant travelling is as tiring as a long working day.

## Visas

For those countries requiring visas, leave enough time for their processing. Many travel agencies have a visa service in which they get the visa in person for you. This is not a free service but considerably quicker and more reliable than applying for a visa by post. For some countries (Nigeria, for instance) getting a visa is notoriously difficult and time consuming.

Although the USA has a visa waiver scheme, this specifically does not cover members of the media working on assignments there. For this, a visa is obligatory. The most common is the I *visa* permitting journalists and film crews to work on US soil on assignments produced solely for a foreign audience. In other words, programmes shot in the States to be transmitted in the UK or the EU only. To apply for a visa, a letter from the employer on headed paper, a photograph, a passport and fee are required. There are other classifications of US visas relevant to the media and these, together with further visa details, can be found either on the US embassy website (www.usembassy.org.uk) or by phoning the Visa Branch directly.

With the modern lightweight cameras small enough to look like home movie camcorders, some researchers are sent to the USA masquerading as tourists and without the relevant visa. This directly contravenes the USA regulations but it happens, especially for cable and satellite personnel. My advice is – get a visa.

The production manager will negotiate all visa applications.

## ATA carnets

An ATA carnet is an international transit certificate, a passport if you like, for tapes and equipment. The international ATA carnet system works between the listed countries ensuring that equipment can pass smoothly, efficiently and quickly between them and also ensures that crews do not have to pay excise duty.

The EU does not require a carnet because goods are free to travel between the countries. At the time of writing, 31 countries recognised the system (including the USA) but as countries are occasionally suspended, it is necessary to check if your country is in the system before setting up a carnet. You need a carnet to *travel through* any of the countries in the system, even if you do not intend to film there.

ATA carnets are issued through the London Chamber of Commerce and Industry. It takes a minimum of 24 hours to process one but if it is a rush job, an express charge will be added to the usual cost. ATA carnets are valid for a year.

Effectively, all the relevant counterfoils in the carnet must be completed correctly and certified by the foreign customs officers when the vouchers are extracted and it is the responsibility of the film crew to check that details are correct as the various customs officials will not admit liability for any errors on their part. Some countries are more rigorous in imposing the conditions than others and a crew may well have all their equipment searched, itemised and ticked off with a veritable slanging match should it appear that the equipment does not correspond. Another time, they may be merely waved through the customs department without a second glance.

Warning – when filming with a carnet, if a member of the production team returns to base early, it is inadvisable to take video tapes or film back with them as this might later cause the film crew problems with an officious customs official. In fact, the general advice is not to list tape or film stock on the carnet at all, although in some locations, unless a huge duty payment is made, it *is* advisable to list the stock on the carnet. For up-to-date information, the London Chamber of Commerce and Industry, *The Knowledge* or the BFI will give advice, as will the production manager.

## Insurance

Many countries, notably the USA, insist on public liability insurance and cover has to be proved before a film permit is granted. The amount to which liability must be proved may be up to five million dollars. (Another reason why some companies dispense with visas.) You may be expected to show the insurance cover (faxing a copy will often suffice) but they may ask for original proof. It is easier to organise this before flying out on location.

Personal insurance for the production team, film crew and equipment will be organised by the production manager who, should you be asked for public liability insurance, will help with the corroboration.

## TRAVEL

### Planes

Whenever possible, the company travel desk will book reputable airlines but because of logistical problems you may occasionally find yourself on Oddjob Airlines. There is not much you can do about this except cross your fingers and take your own food and water.

### Airport security

The same security systems are in place for travelling with a film crew as they are for going on holiday. Most airports insist on X-raying all goods whether they are travelling by freight or accompanied by passengers.

Modern security x-ray machines at ports and airports are not supposed to harm film. They do not affect videotape. For modern countries, you should be safe. For poorer countries, their systems might still cause problems and, under these circumstances it is still inadvisable to take film through these machines. The carnet system should ensure that.

Everyone is aware of the restricted articles list (fireworks – including party poppers and crackers – knives, guns – including toy guns – paint, chemicals) and there are also certain personal luggage articles that, because of the pressurised cabins, should not been taken on board as hand baggage. These include all aerosols including shaving foam and hair spray.

Electrical appliances, on the other hand, are preferably carried in hand baggage so that they can be identified on the X-ray machines on departure. American Airlines, however, ban electric games, toys with remote controls, radios and television sets anywhere on the plane. There has been a lot of media publicity recently about the use of mobile phones and laptop computers on planes (especially on take-off and landing) and on no account should these be used during the flight until permitted as they interfere with airplanes' flight systems. If unsure, phone the airline in advance especially as rules change so quickly nowadays.

For articles on the restricted list, you need to speak to a specialist freight agent.

## Trains

On the few occasions when it is necessary to travel by train whilst abroad, it is likely you will be booked into First Class. This is essential in developing countries if only for hygiene and safety's sake where there may be little apparent difference between our standard class and their first.

## Hotels

Television personnel stay in good hotels. There are several reasons for this: a reliable communications system, phones in rooms and often computer access, early and late catering facilities (hopefully hygienic), laundry facilities, en-suite bathrooms and comfortable lodgings.

When you are working hard and for long hours, you don't want to sleep in a fleapit, and you need to be readily contactable. Having said this, the urban myths are legendary (dead bodies in a New York hotel bed). However, should you be working on an off-the-beaten-track programme à la Michael Wood/Michael Palin, creature comforts will, of necessity, be few.

When slumming it with the jet set, remember to take suitable clothing for the restaurant – jacket and tie for the men, and a dress for the women. No jeans here.

## Luggage

This is my personal advice. If you are a frequent traveller you may disagree with me and have your own essential items to add.

- Travel as light as you can. Use hotel laundry services.
- Pack a rigid suitcase with wheels attached. (A rigid case dissuades petty theft and slashing.)
- Attention is drawn to designer luggage – don't use it.
- Do not take anything valuable or sentimental or which cannot be replaced.

Essentials:

- passport;

- photocopied passport details kept separately;

- spare passport-sized photographs;

- insurance details and emergency phone numbers including home phone numbers of colleagues back at base;

- copies of inoculation certificates (kept with passport);

- credit cards (one or two only). Get your employer to issue you with a company card to which all your filming expenses are charged;

- money (a few foreign notes but the majority in traveller's cheques), spare coins are invaluable for phones abroad;

- tickets if travelling solo. If travelling in a group, they may be held by the production manager or PA;

- body belt to keep the above safe;

- travel alarm clock;

- frequent travellers swear by two watches, one set at local time and one at Greenwich Mean Time;

- personal medical kit for countries with high AIDS figures;

- personal medical supplies (i.e. condoms, contraceptive pills, prescribed drugs, anti-diarrhoea preparation, but see notes on diarrhoea);

- localised medical supplies such as malarial prophylactics;

- antibiotic/antiseptic wipes;

- toilet roll/travel tissues for noses/bottoms – flat boxes are convenient;

- bottled water for long plane journeys;

- phone card;

- small inflatable travel pillow.

I store most of the above permanently in a suitcase so that they don't get mislaid between trips. The passports and papers are kept separately.

## Film crew tips

- Go to the airport gate at *final*, final call. The flight will not leave without you. I can't recommend this – the exact closing time at the gate varies from airline to airline. British Airways will refuse entry 10 minutes before the flight is due to leave.

- At immigration/port of entry, join a queue with families in it. Immigration Officers deal with several people at once and the queues move quicker.

- Do not cross the white line when queuing up for immigration. This makes security personnel nervous and some are armed with automatic weapons.

- Travel as light as possible. (This from a crew with up to 80 packages of cameras and lenses.)

## WHILE YOU ARE THERE

### Bribes

Some countries are notorious for bribery. Nigeria is one of these. Television companies, production managers and facilitators are all well aware of the practice that, although supposedly outlawed, is very much in existence. Do not initiate bribery yourself. When you come home and fill in your expenses claims form, bribery payments are listed as *incidentals* or whatever the accounts department recommend you to put down. You won't, of course, have a receipt!

### Facilitators

When working in an unfamiliar country, it helps to have on-the-ground help. The United States (and the UK, too, to aid crews working here) have film offices in many states offering, on the whole, free services, although certain requirements must be paid for.

The justification of these film offices is to provide local income and employment by encouraging film companies to shoot in their region. A large film boosts an area's income by millions of pounds (or dollars) not just by the amount of money spent in hotels and restaurants and the employment of local crewmembers and extras during filming but by the surge in tourism afterwards.

The service provided by US Film Offices depends on the office and ranges from recommending hotels and restaurants to suggesting and shortlisting locations, accompanying production personnel on recces or taking the production crew around the various governmental departments to arrange film licences. In other words, providing an extremely helpful and time-cutting service.

The Las Vegas office, for example, negotiated for me: filming in casinos (many are hesitant to admit film crews), stretch limos and a couple prepared to be filmed getting married in a wedding chapel. We paid for the hire of the limo, the cost of the wedding (as a good-will gesture) and the film licence. The Vegas Film Production services were free. In their terms, ours was a relatively small production. In a country where the second largest industry (after aeronautics) is film production, everyone is used to film crews on the streets, the closing of entire streets and a large police security presence. But it costs. And it costs a bomb. A facilitator is invaluable when organising all this but the production covers the cost of the road closure, insurance, security presence, *et al.* The cost of a licence to film in the US is on a sliding scale depending on how much disruption is caused. The minimum fee is very low. The maximum? Filming *Honey, I Blew Up The Kid* which involved closing off Downtown Las Vegas, filled the city's coffers by several million dollars.

Once again, if your production has a location manager they will organise many of these commitments, but I organised a foreign shoot through the not inconsiderable help from various film offices.

A point to consider: film offices are manned by a minimum number of people so treat them with courtesy and respect – they have homes to go to, too.

For countries less organised than the States, it is a good idea to find a similar facilitator who will smooth your passage through the minefield of different laws and customs. Contacts for foreign facilitators can be found in *The Knowledge*. Professional facilitators are paid for their assistance.

Tourist Offices are usually very obliging but this is a sideline to their job. Tourist Agencies, by their very nature, are also free. They are, however, less au fait with the specific problems of filming and more relaxed about schedules than film crews. Embassies may be approached but treat these very cautiously.

Another line to pursue are stringers. These are freelance crew: cameramen, sound recordists, directors working in their own countries earning their daily bread by submitting stories to news agencies such as Reuters. Their extensive local knowledge combined with the benefit of understanding problems associated with filming is invaluable. They are paid for their assistance as this is how they make their living.

## HEALTH AND SAFETY

Some citizens in the USA have the preconceived idea that life in the UK is significantly more dangerous than that in the States. To us, it's completely the opposite.

Although it is extremely doubtful that you would be expected to film in a dangerous area, the Foreign Office issues advice with a constantly updated list of which countries offer most risk to travellers and currently their 'don't visit at any cost' areas include twenty dangerous zones. Call them for advice or visit their website on www.fco.gov.uk/travel. If the Foreign Office is warning against visiting a country, you must consider your decision very carefully, especially if you are travelling alone.

Rape is an increasing risk for women in some countries, including Europe, and it has become apparent recently that women accompanied by a man are just as much at risk as a woman on her own.

Certain countries have dress expectations. In Muslim countries, women (even those on film crews) are expected to dress modestly. Be aware that you will have fewer problems if you wear a shalwar kameez or similar clothing worn by the local women, and that shorts, even though it is hot, will be seen as insensitive and provocative.

Dietary laws should be respected. Alcohol, for instance, is forbidden in certain countries and what appear to us to be peculiar regulations relating to the purchase and drinking of alcohol apply locally in the USA as well.

## Penalties for law infringement

In some parts of the world, the penalties for infringing the alcohol laws can be severe and it is better safe than sorry under such circumstances.

As for illegal drugs, the penalties for drug offences are devastatingly harsh. Everyone knows that in Thailand the death sentence is *automatic* for drug traffickers, but India has a mandatory ten-year prison sentence for anyone caught with more than 10 grams of cannabis. Being found in possession of cocaine in Spain results in a sentence of between nine and fourteen years.

There are other less well-known offences. Photographing shrines and temples in Sri Lanka is allowed with prior permission but posing with religious statues is not. If your visa runs out in Nepal, there is a £2,600 fine or ten years in jail.

As there is no defence in pleading ignorance, check with the Foreign Office or the local national tourist office beforehand.

## Illness

Diarrhoea and food poisoning are potentially your worst enemies. My worst case of food poisoning was from a popular casino in Las Vegas so it can happen anywhere.

Tips on how to avoid and treat diarrhoea and food poisoning are:

- eat what the locals eat, i.e. fresh food cooked fast. When in a vegetarian country, don't eat meat as they are unused to storing or cooking it;

- avoid shellfish;

- eating yoghurt and banana every morning works well in preventing diarrhoea (according to several film crews I have worked with);

- avoid salads unless you are sure of the source and peel fruit before eating;

- drink bottled water and watch the cap being removed. It is not unknown for bottles to be refilled and resold;

- avoid ice in drinks. The water source may be contaminated;

- avoid anti-diarrhoea remedies unless absolutely necessary – if affected, rehydrate with a proprietary brand of sugar and salts (take your own supply from the UK) and drink plenty of bottled water.

This is not a failsafe guide but should help stave off the worst.

## Malaria, hepatitis, etc.

These are endemic in some parts of the world. Your local Health Centre, Travel Clinic (and travel desk) will advise you of the nasty bugs you are letting yourself in for. Take a trip to your Health Centre or Travel Clinic for the relevant jabs, pills and potions and ensure you follow the instructions exactly.

Some potentially fatal illnesses like malaria can manifest themselves weeks after your return home and it is essential to continue taking the prophylactics for the prescribed amount of time. The malaria parasite is becoming resistant to certain prophylactics and you must take advice on which drug works in which area.

## Advice for flights, especially long-haul

- Restrict your alcohol intake. Don't be tempted by the free alcohol; it reacts badly with your body in pressurised conditions. Troublemakers are often arrested on landing.

- Crews are notoriously boisterous. If you are travelling with the crew, respect the other passengers.

- Carry a bottle of mineral water in your hand baggage and drink it.

- A lot of attention has been drawn recently to deep vein thrombosis, the so-called economy class syndrome. Current advice for long flights is to drink lots of water, remove your shoes and take frequent strolls up and down the cabin. If there isn't room, even wiggling your toes and turning your ankles is better than nothing. The benefit of taking an aspirin beforehand has also been suggested. It is worth speaking to the company doctor for up-to-date guidance.

## Sexual health

Everyone is aware of the risk of AIDS, hepatitis and sexually-transmitted diseases so either refrain from sex or ensure you have adequate protection. Take your own condoms. In some cultures, sexual activity outside marriage is prohibited and not only may it incur disapprobation but it may also be difficult to procure contraceptives locally. On all counts, the best protection is celibacy.

## RELATIONSHIP WARNING

Whenever I get home after a long spell of hotel food, I tuck in to egg and chips. Friends of mine enjoy beans on toast. This may appear a trite reason for relationship breakdowns but, after several weeks away when the left-at-home partner has dealt with faulty washing machines and sick children, they may wish to celebrate your return with a meal out when all you want is nursery food. Add the stress and strain of filming, the close relationships forged on location, and you can understand that holding on to a relationship can be difficult to achieve without tact, humour and compromise.

## FINALLY

- Never be persuaded to carry packages for somebody else.

- Do not make jokes at check-in about having a bomb or not having packed your own case.

- Reconfirm your return flight and any others if the airline recommends it.

- Keep all your receipts.

## ORGANISATIONS

The Foreign Office, www.fco.gov.uk/travel.

# 10
# Radio research

Although the number of radio stations is expanding day by day, radio is, in many respects, the Cinderella of the media. Compared to television, there is a relatively small audience and the fewest number of listeners is that for local radio stations. Because the audiences are so small, the budgets are minuscule, there is no money for pre-production and everything is required *now*.

Fewer researchers work in radio than in television and it is more of a multi-skilled medium. The radio researcher is mainly found in the BBC Radios 1 to 5 and on local stations working on documentaries, current affairs and special interest programmes, very often as a pool supplying ideas for several programmes at once. It is quite common for the producer to do their own research or, especially in local radio, for the researcher to produce and present packages they have researched. Not only this, but researchers and producers commonly operate their own recording equipment and edit the packages back at base. In other words, if you become a radio researcher

a   you may be being groomed for a radio producer's job;

b   you must be prepared to operate all the equipment yourself. Engineers are only there to stop you falling off air.

Local radio is very audience focused. The audience in Northampton is only interested in people and stories specific to their particular area. They listen because it is local and they don't care what is happening twenty miles down the road. This is the difference between programmes made for local consumption and those directed at a national audience.

There are a few national independent radio stations, Classic FM, Talk FM and several who transmit locally but are part of a national group. The BBC, of course, has many local radio stations together with the five national ones transmitting over the entire network. A BBC network programme should use stories originating from all over the country, and is expected to do so as it is funded by licence payers.

The obvious difference between radio and television is, to quote the old saying, 'the pictures are better on radio'. Paradoxically, this can be beneficial and removes many restrictions.

It is the voice that counts. Who cares what they look like? Who cares what they are wearing? Research, however, corroborates that a monotonous voice switches off the audience quicker than anything else, and the importance of an articulate speaker becomes paramount.

The benefits of working without pictures are:

- **Editorial**
  A major criticism of television news recently is that a story appears because of the pictures and not because of its journalistic content. No pictures – no story. In comparison, radio is editorially led. What counts is that the story is journalistically newsworthy. It doesn't require visuals. The wider dimension is achieved by verbal contributions from people other than the presenter. For Radio 1's *Newsbeat* bulletins, the sound bite, imported from TV, is becoming more prevalent. If circumstances dictate that it is impossible to provide an external voice, the presenter's script may be enough.

- **Immediacy**
  Stories can be virtually immediate. Take the Paddington rail crash. The immensity of it was revealed over mobile phones by several journalists who had been on the train or near enough to have heard the crash. Their phone calls were technically of 'non-broadcast quality' but this was superseded by the immediacy, newsworthiness and tragedy of the situation.

- **Global stories**
  Paradoxically, even though radio has considerably less money to spend, stories need not be dropped because they are on the other side of the world. A phone line is all that is needed for transmission. With no pictures to find, no film crew to pay, stories are economically feasible. Setting up the phone lines can, however, be difficult as shown by the frequent problems Radio 4 has.

## Radio personnel

Because radio is a more compact medium than television, there is a smaller range of jobs. Personnel moving from radio to television are often horrified to find how many extra people are needed.

The BBC is funded by the licence fee and does not have advertisements. This statement may appear simplistic but has an integral affect on radio output and the jobs in the BBC and independent radio stations. In other words, people in independent radio sell airtime to advertisers and the *traffic* department checks they are played at the correct time so the advertisers pay their bills. Programme making is almost a secondary activity which is why so many independent radio stations play music interrupted by (inane) chat. Although it is cheap and relies on minimum production personnel, it must, of course, deliver to the target audience or the advertisers won't buy airtime. The news is bought in from IRN (Independent Radio News). The producers for independent radio stations invariably do their own research, although a station assistant may be employed to help out.

Depending on the station (BBC or independent) and its output, there will be producers, researchers, journalists/reporters, presenters/disc jockeys, station assistants, broadcast assistants (the equivalent of a PA in television), music editors (to devise the play list of music for music programmes), the promotions department, the traffic department and marketing departments. The last three do not produce programmes.

## The role of the researcher in radio

This depends on the type of programme the researcher is working on: magazine/chat shows, music/chat shows, the news (which tends to employ journalists), features, drama and sport.

The major component of the researcher's job, just as in television, is to find contributors and to suggest stories, but, because of the budgetary constraints, there is less time. A few hours is often all the notice that is given. Advice on finding contributors is found in Chapter 4. As has already been mentioned, the delineation between the role of the producer and the researcher is much narrower in radio. Producers often do their own research, researchers may produce and act as presenter.

Effectively, this means that anyone working in radio must speak clearly and have a good microphone voice (often tested at interview). Unlike television which only appears to employ the beautiful people, those in radio can be more homely in appearance. Regional accents are no longer frowned on, even in the BBC, and the BBC Pronunciation Unit can help with difficult and controversial words. The radio researcher is more likely than their television counterpart to conduct their own interviews, edit them as well as script and edit promotional material such as trails. Even those working for Radio 4 are expected to do this. If interviews are conducted over the phone, then researchers may well set up an ISDN link with the engineers.

## Phone links

ISDN lines (Integrated Services over a Digital Network) are a better and faster digital signal which can be used for both voice and non-voice data over the public telephone system. It does not have the crackle of standard telephone lines but, of course, is more expensive and your budget may not cover the cost. In obscure parts of the world, especially Third World countries, ISDN lines are few and far between.

The BBC generally regards the broadcast quality of phone lines as unacceptable but, if used as a last resort, are permitted for a short period of time. If at all possible, use a studio or OB vehicle rather than a phone line. 'Down the line' recordings can be fraught with difficulty and notoriously difficult to set up especially when staffed by freelance operators at the other end who do not know the system.

## The use of music in radio

Using music and musicians is not such a problem for radio researchers as it is for those working in television.

Radio's relationship with music is symbiotic. Most commercial recording agreements allow almost unconditional use of music on radio and the only issue that may arise is one of moral rights. As composers and musicians rarely assert the moral rights clause in their agreements until they have become established and well known, this is only likely to affect the bigger bands.

If a band or orchestra is transmitted live, no mechanical recording takes place and therefore the MCPS are not involved. The composer and publisher's rights are covered by the PRS blanket agreement and as long as you have the copyright details, there is little else to worry about. The safe arrival and set up of the musicians and the MU fees are all that is left to consider. The technical quality of the sound is the province of the engineering department.

Where the playlist system is in place (in which programmers dictate the list and order of the music) most paperwork, particularly for Radio 1, is done electronically and all that must be reported is the music played and tracks omitted through lack of time. In the absence of a broadcast assistant (BA) nowadays, the producer or researcher tend to do the paperwork.

## Sound archives

Sound archives may be required for inclusion in speech packages. The BBC has a huge sound archive as does the British Library. Because of the nature of sound archives, the BBC is geared up for research for both independent producers and those within the BBC. There is an in-house charge for archive use.

## Drama clips

As in television, the use of drama extracts and how much it costs depends on the agreements with Equity and the BBC or whoever made the original recording. There are separate rates for extracts, consents from the performers may have to be agreed (refer to Chapter 5), and if performances are repeated after a certain time, the old agreements may be 'out of time', meaning that a new agreement will have to be made. This is all the province of the casting department.

## Health and safety

Cutting and splicing tape with razor blades and playing out spools is virtually obsolete. Most stations edit digitally on SADIE and Protools and record on DAT or minidisk recorders. Apart from the safety rules when working with electricity, there are few other hazards.

For going on recces and meeting potential contributors, refer to Chapters 4 and 8 as the health and safety issues are similar.

## FURTHER READING

Radio Academy Yearbook, The Radio Academy, 5 Market Place, London W1N 7AH, Tel 020 7255 2010, e-mail: info@radacad.demon.co.uk. www.radacad.demon.co.uk.
Beaman, Jim, *Interviewing for Radio*, Routledge, 2000.
Chantler, Paul and Harris, Sim, *Local Radio Journalism*, Focal Press, 1997.
Crisell, Andrew, *Understanding Radio*, Routledge, 2nd edn, 1994.
Douglas, Lawrie and Kinsey, Marie (eds), *Guide to Commercial Radio Journalism*, Focal Press, 1997.
McLeish, Robert, *Radio Production*, Focal Press, 4th edn, 1999.
Wilby, Pete and Conroy, Andy, *The Radio Handbook*, Routledge, 1994.

## ORGANISATION

Radio Authority, Holbrook House, 14 Great Queen Street, Holborn, London WC2B 5DG, Tel 020 7430 2724.

# 11
# A summary of legal issues

For ease of reference, I have put this chapter's contents in alphabetical order. As the law may change after this book is published it is recommended that you keep up to date with current legislation. The various guidelines (BSC, ITC, RA) are also revised from time to time and, if in doubt, refer directly to them. The addresses of the organisations concerned are found in the Appendix. The main legal issues to worry about are those of filming permission, copyright (covered in Chapter 12) and libel.

## ACCURACY

This is fundamental to the media, whether it be programme making for radio, television or for the press and the magnitude of its importance cannot be stressed enough. The BBC's guidelines state:

> Research for all programmes must be thorough. We must be prepared to check, cross-check and seek advice, to ensure this. Wherever possible we should gather information first-hand by being there ourselves or, where that is not possible, by talking to those who were.
>
> (*BBC Producers' Guidelines*, Chapter 2:
> Impartiality and Accuracy Part two: accuracy. 1 General)

Although you cannot be taken to court for 'getting it wrong' there are occasions where a lack of accuracy (or substantial proof of it) can lead to litigation; libel is the most obvious.

## BLASPHEMY

The laws on blasphemy are ancient and, many argue, anachronistic, as they are solely concerned with Christianity when they should also, in our multi-ethnic society, include other religions. The furore which followed the publication of Salman Rushdie's *The Satanic Verses* is a case in point.

The BSC, in clause 31 of their codes of conduct, refers specifically to offences against religious sensibilities and the use of swear words.

## CHEQUE-BOOK JOURNALISM

This is not illegal at the moment (the government has plans to make it so) but is heavily frowned upon by the *NUJ Code of Conduct* and other voluntary guidelines. There have been some infamous cases recently whereby prominent trial witnesses have been promised payment according to the outcome – marginally close to contravening the laws of contempt.

## CHILDREN

### Appearing in programmes

It is a legal requirement that children under sixteen do not take time out of school. For children appearing in programmes during school hours, see Chapter 4.

Legislation governs the number of hours and the type of employment that children can take. In some cases, there are restrictions up to the age of eighteen. The ITC insists that *under no circumstances may children be put at moral or physical risk* (ITC *Programme Code: 6. Other Legal Matters 6.4* Appearances by children in programmes).

The Protection of Children Act 1978, makes it an offence to take indecent photographs, videos or film of children under sixteen or for children to take part in such material even when their own role is not indecent. Under such circumstances, it is also illegal for actors over sixteen to portray under-age children.

For further guidance, see the BSC, ITC and RA guidelines.

### Children as offenders or victims

Under the Children and Young Persons Acts 1933 and 1967 (England and Wales) it is an offence to publish the names and addresses of children under seventeen who are involved in court proceedings or to publish any information which may lead to their identity being revealed. Similar rulings apply to Scotland and Northern Ireland. Broadcasting such information is therefore prohibited unless a judge lifts the restriction.

### Children as viewers

All the regulatory bodies are keen to ensure that children are not upset or inadvertently influenced by programmes aimed at them. The use of bad language before the watershed (generally accepted as 9 p.m. until 5 a.m.) and especially during programmes specifically aimed at them is a case in point but so is the choice of subject matter. Violence, the use of guns and offensive weapons, crime, drugs and solvent abuse, anything harmful that may be imitated, must not be broadcast when children are listening or watching.

## Contempt of court

The reason why video cameras are not permitted in trials at British courts is because of the law of contempt which places 'a temporary embargo on the publication or broadcast of information which might influence the course of judicial proceedings' (*ITC Programme Code:* 6. Other Legal Matters 6.2 Contempt of court).

Contempt of court is a criminal offence with a maximum penalty of two years' imprisonment and an unlimited fine. It is not only people who can be in breach of this law, but also broadcasts which, if they are found to interfere with the course of justice (by vilifying a defendant for instance) can constitute contempt.

Legal advice should be sought if there is a risk that a comment, photograph or interview is in contempt of court.

## CONTRACTS

An employment contract is binding by law. The casting and personnel departments are obviously the first port of call for any employment queries.

## DEFAMATION; LIBEL AND SLANDER

Effectively, libel is when a defamatory statement is published or broadcast. Slander is when a defamatory statement is spoken. The reason why television and radio defamation is termed libel (and not slander) is because it is in a permanent form.

Current affairs and news programmes are most likely to be faced with issues of libel but gossip in chat shows may also cause concern. When in doubt, the first stop is to refer the problematic statement to the producer. When in further doubt, the producer will refer on to a higher authority. All television companies have media lawyers whose province covers libel and when in doubt, the script or transcript of a pre-recorded interview can be referred on to the lawyer. Lawyers are over-protective and err on the side of caution so that an 'exciting gritty, controversial' programme may become weak and toothless.

Lines in the commentary may explain that a contributor's contentious opinion is not that of the programme maker. However, if the situation blows up out of all proportion, the producer and the production company may be sued for compensation.

*The ITC Programme Code:* 6. Other Legal Matters, 6.1, although only a rough guide to the law of defamation in England and Wales, alerts producers to situations where legal advice is required before transmission.

## D-NOTICES – DEFENCE ADVISORY NOTES AND THE OFFICIAL SECRETS ACTS

There may be times when a television programme touches on matters of national security. Programme makers working in this province need to be aware of the Official Secrets Acts of 1911 and 1989.

Defence Advisory Notes, 'D-notices' for short, are issued by the Defence, Press and Broadcasting Advisory Committee and are designed to advise the media that if they broadcast or publish certain information, it may damage national security. They are voluntary notices and do not have the force of law, however; even if an item is cleared from a D-notice, there still might be a legal risk should the item be transmitted.

Senior executives will be involved with all decisions should a D-notice be applied.

## ETHNIC MINORITIES

The ITC code states that 'racist terms should be avoided. Their inclusion is acceptable only where it can be clearly justified within the context of the programme' (*ITC Programme Code:* 1. Offence to Good Taste and Decency, Portrayal of Violence, etc. 1.9 Treatment of minorities 1.9(i) Ethnic minorities). It continues to say that stereotypes should be avoided and depictions should 'give a fair reflection of the contribution of all races to society'. The BSC enforces this.

It is an offence to incite racial hatred. Sections 21 and 22 of the Race Relations Act 1976 refer specifically to broadcasting.

## IMPARTIALITY AND BIAS

All regulatory bodies regard impartiality as vital. This issue is discussed in many places throughout this book. The codes of conduct explain further.

## INSURANCE

Many television companies have suddenly woken up to their liability both towards their staff, contributors and the general public. Gone are the days, I hope, when a member of the general public embarks on a dangerous stunt when, if there is a nasty accident, it is discovered that there was no insurance. Risk assessment is crucial.

Insurance and health and safety have been covered in several chapters; the HSE can give plentiful guidance and there are some excellent books on the subject.

## LANGUAGE AND OBSCENITY

Television and radio is often criticised for the use of bad language. The watershed curtails the use of unsuitable subject matter, obscene language and violence before 9 p.m. (the time is under review) but there are increasing complaints that sexual and moral topics unsuitable for family viewing are creeping into daytime scheduling in soap operas and daytime shows like *This Morning*, *Oprah*, *Ricki Lake* and *Jerry Springer*.

The ITC states:

> There is no absolute ban on the use of bad language. But many people are offended, some of them deeply, by the use of bad language, including expletives with a religious (and not only Christian) association . . . gratuitous use of bad language must be avoided.
>
> (*ITC Programme Code:* 1. Offence to Good Taste and Decency,
> Portrayal of Violence, etc. 1.4 language)

It adds that programmes specially designed for children should not contain bad language at all and that the most offensive language should only be included post 9 p.m. having been approved at a senior level beforehand.

Radio 4 is not averse to including four-letter words in its daytime drama and current affairs programmes.

The same guidelines apply to sex and nudity but 'Of the greatest concern are scenes of non-consensual sexual portrayal, including rape, and particularly where there is graphic physical detail or the action is to any degree prolonged' (*ITC Programme Code:* 1. Offence to Good Taste and Decency, Portrayal of Violence, etc. 1.5 Sex and nudity). In other words, if the scenes are portrayed with tact and discretion and can be defended as integral to the programme, and as long as sexual intercourse isn't represented before 9 p.m., these can be transmitted. Again, approval must be sought from a senior executive.

## PRIVACY

According to Articles 8 and 10 of the European Convention on Human Rights, everyone has a right to privacy for private and family life and the right to freedom of expression, and this was incorporated into UK law in the Human Rights Act 1998. This legislation is obviously integral to all codes of practice which give guidance on the use of recording telephone interviews, hidden microphones and cameras, scenes of extreme suffering and distress, interviewing children, set-up situations, interviews without prior arrangement and video news releases.

## RELEASE FORMS AND PERMISSION TO FILM

This is widely covered in Chapter 8, 'Filming on location'. See also the codes of practice.

## FURTHER READING

Baker, Rhonda, *Media Law*, Routledge, 1994.

# 12
# Copyright

Media products often use previously recorded material such as 'archive' footage, music to add atmosphere, clips from feature films, news and so on. Without the inclusion of these, the product would be very bare, basic and with no extra dimension.

However, whoever writes a poem, book, software, takes a photograph, composes music, paints a picture or creates a sculpture has rights because they created it. Anything that effectively has been created is 'owned' by someone who must be paid for the right to reproduce it. Hence the 'right to copy' or *copyright*.

Copyright can be transferred by inheritance or by being bought and sold, but some of the rights themselves may be retained and this is what makes the copyright issue so complicated.

According to the Copyright, Designs and Patents Act 1988 which replaced the Copyright Act 1956, the categories of works which are the subject of copyright protection include:

a   original literary, dramatic, musical or artistic works;

b   sound recordings, films, broadcasts or cable programmes; and

c   typographical arrangements of published editions.

In 1996, European legislation extended the length of copyright from 50 years to 70 years after the death of the author. However, the copyright for sound recordings and broadcasts remains at 50 years.

Ideas cannot be copyrighted. Inevitably, most ideas have been thought of before, but try telling someone that. Television stations are always taking calls from members of the public insisting that they 'spoke to someone at your television studio last week/month' with the same idea and format that they are now seeing on the screen. Even though the programme had been in production for several months and had been put forward to the programme committee a year before that, the caller still argues that their idea has been stolen.

## PUBLIC DOMAIN

Anything out of copyright is technically in the public domain and can be used without payment.

## PIRATE COPIES

It is estimated that 90 per cent of video cassettes in the Far East are pirate copies and that there are 21 million pirated tapes in British homes. This costs the British film industry about £200 million a year in lost revenue and the same figure is lost to British publishers and their authors by unauthorised publishing of books in Russia and China.

Basically, the money made from illegal copying goes into the back pocket of the pirates and not back into industry where the sale of videos, cinema tickets and CDs ensures more films and albums and ultimately more employment.

What most people fail to realise is that not only is it illegal to make, import, sell, hire or distribute any copies which have infringed copyright, it is also illegal to own them.

## THE INTERNET

Rumour or supposition maintains that everything on the Internet is copyright free. This is not true.

Annually, billions of pounds are lost to authors, publishers, filmmakers and the music industry via the Internet.

At the moment, although technology is increasingly improving, pictures, music, film clips, indeed anything downloaded from the Internet, is not of broadcast quality. Find useful sources by all means, but then get the original material from the copyright owner, clear the rights and broadcast legally. The problem lies in ascertaining who is the copyright holder. So much on the Web has been scanned in, sourced from other websites and copied that a number of sources may claim ownership or that it is copyright-free. Reputable and official sites are safer than most but when in doubt, phone.

The copyright on computer-generated works lasts for 50 years.

## PHOTOCOPYING

Over the past few years, the Copyright Licensing Agency (CLA) and the

Authors' Licensing and Collecting Society (ALCS) have attempted to raise the profile of the illegality of wholesale photocopying. The ALCS and CLA act as collecting and redistribution agencies. However, photocopying is difficult to police and many companies, not surprisingly, prefer to risk prosecution.

## NAMES

There is no copyright on a name or title. Trademarks are an exception and some programme titles have been trademarked. Also beware of using characters' names from *Coronation Street* or other such programmes. The BBC successfully sued British Telecom for using several *EastEnders* actors, 'playing themselves' in an advert. The BBC claimed that by using the actors collectively, they were seen as soap opera characters not actors.

## NOVELS, POETRY, PLAYS AND THE PRINTED WORD

Adapting novels for the screen and the purchase of the rights to do so are not in the province of the researcher. However, quoting from novels, poetry or plays may well be.

If a work is old enough to be out of copyright and in public domain, this affords no problem whatsoever. However, if the intention is to film the text and put that on screen, the typography of the book may be in copyright depending on when the book was printed. In other words, Charles Dickens' work is out of copyright but the typeface of the latest Penguin edition of *Oliver Twist* and the preface is not.

Similarly, quoting Wordsworth's *Daffodils* is fine, but quoting something where the author has died within the last 70 years is not. The fees for quoting poetry depend on how many lines are to be used, the importance or fame of the poet and the transmission area. A programme intended for sale abroad will be charged more than a local programme. Refer to the publisher for permission to quote.

Letters are different. The letter itself belongs to the recipient but the copyright belongs to the writer. However, if the letters have been assigned to a library then the library is the owner. Quoting from a letter requires a minimum of at least two phone calls and still may not be straightforward.

Both the playwright and the publisher have a vested interest in the fees for quoting from plays. J.M. Barrie, the author of *Peter Pan*, left the rights to the Great Ormond Street Hospital for Sick Children. As a huge amount of the hospital's income was derived from *Peter Pan*, it took an Act of Parliament to renew the copyright and ensure the continuance of the royalties.

Some authors, notably Irving Berlin (although a composer) have ensured that the lyrics of their songs cannot be parodied or treated derogatorily. This is the right of integrity.

See Chapter 7 for more information on music copyright.

See Chapter 5, for more information on copyright for television programmes, feature films, sport, photographs, pictures, paintings/printed archive material such as old sketches and works of art.

## SOUND EFFECTS/SOUND RECORDINGS

When the 1996 EU legislation extended the copyright cover from 50 to 70 years, it specifically omitted sound recordings and cable and television broadcasts. In other words, the copyright for sound recordings and broadcasts still only lasts for 50 years.

## COIN OF THE REALM

It is illegal to reproduce or photocopy bank notes or coin of the realm as this infringes copyright. For example, if a large facsimile bank note is required, permission must be sought from the Bank of England.

## COMPANY LOGOS, TRADEMARKS, DISNEY CHARACTERS, VIDEO GAMES, DESIGNS

Unlike copyright, trademarks go on forever; consider the trademark Coca-Cola, reputedly the most famous and international logo in the world, and over a century old. Trademarks can be registered and once registered, last forever. Coca Cola has not only registered its name as a trademark but also registered the design of the bottle.

Video game characters and images such as Lara Croft and Pokémon are trademarked. Characters invented by Disney, for instance, are all licensed. Thus, if a clothing company wants to put Disney's Snow White on its pyjamas, they have to clear copyright with Disney and buy a licence to reproduce the character. These marketing off-shoots are extremely lucrative. The anomaly is, of course, that Snow White, being a fairy tale, is in public domain but the Disney image of her isn't.

To show one of these characters on television (unless governed by the fair dealing rules, see p. 151) is reproducing a trademark, and should be cleared with a fee paid if required.

Using company logos such as the shell of the eponymous oil company in investigative documentaries and news programmes is an exception to copyright infringement as it is fair dealing for the purpose of criticism or reporting current events.

Designs and architectural drawings are covered by copyright and therefore need to be cleared in the usual way.

## SUMMARY

- Copyright is extremely complicated and on any but the simplest issues, professional advice is *always* required.

## FURTHER READING

Flint, *A User's Guide to Copyright*, Butterworths, 4th edn, London, 1997.
Laddie, Prescott and Vitoria, *The Modern Law of Copyright*, Butterworths, 2nd edn, 1995.
Copyright Designs and Patents Act 1988, Stationery Office.
The Duration of Copyright and Rights in Performances Regulations, 1995 (SI 1995 No. 3297).
The Patent Office supplies a short pamphlet titled *Basic Facts, Copyright.*

Short articles on copyright are found in:
*The Knowledge* – music copyright.
*Check Book*, British Film Commission.
*The Writers' and Artists' Yearbook*, A & C Black.

Organisations are listed in Appendix 3.

# Appendix 1
# Guidelines

## BROADCASTING STANDARDS COMMISSION

This was set up in 1996 to act as the statutory governing body over standards and fairness in broadcasting, and is the only organisation to cover television and radio, terrestrial and satellite, cable and digital. It has three main tasks: producing codes of conduct relating to standards and fairness, considering and adjudicating complaints and monitoring, researching and reporting on standards and fairness in broadcasting.

The codes can be downloaded from the Internet and they cover:

* fairness, including *inter alia* correction and apology;

* privacy, including the use of hidden microphones and cameras, telephone calls, doorstepping, children and more;

* scheduling, including the watershed, programme repeats, trails, advertisement labelling and warnings;

* taste and decency, including swearing, offences against religious sensibilities, lyrics, race, alcohol and smoking, stereotypes and archive material, etc.;

* portrayal of violence in different genres.

For further information, see their website at www.bsc.org.uk. Broadcasting Standards Commission, 7 The Sanctuary, London SW1P 3JS, Tel 020 7808 1000.

## ITC PROGRAMME CODE

Contents include:

* Offence to Good Taste and Decency, Portrayal of Violence etc.,

* Privacy, Gathering of Information.

- Impartiality.

- Party Political and Parliamentary Broadcasting.

- Terrorism, Crime, Antisocial Behaviour, etc.

- Other Legal Matters.

- Images of Very Brief Duration.

- Charitable Appeals and Publicity for Charities.

- Religion.

- Other Programme Matters.

- Communication with the Public.

- Extract from the Broadcasting Act 1990.

- Programmes at the Time of Elections.

## ITC CODE OF PROGRAMME SPONSORSHIP

Programme researchers will primarily be concerned with Part B of this code –
*The ITC Rules Concerning Advertiser Involvement in Programmes.* This effectively covers the following points:

- product placement;

- undue prominence;

- similarity between programmes and advertising;

- advertiser references in game shows and viewer competitions;

- coverage of events;

- timing and information services;

- sponsored support material.

Copies can be obtained from the ITC or their website www.itc.org.uk.

## RADIO AUTHORITY PROGRAMME CODE

Contents include:

- taste, decency, offence to public feeling and the portrayal of violence;

- accuracy;

- privacy and gathering of information;

- crime, terrorism and anti-social behaviour;

- legal matters;

- appeals for donations;

- religious and other spiritual or ethereal matters;

- obituary and royalty;

- competitions and premium rate telephone services;

- public accountability;

- programme sponsorship code;

- appendices with sections from the Broadcasting Act 1990, the Broadcasting Standards Commission and the Law in Scotland and Northern Ireland.

## RADIO AUTHORITY NEWS AND CURRENT AFFAIRS CODE

Contents include:

- undue prominence and impartiality;

- party politics, politicians and programmes;

- appendices with the relevant sections from the Broadcasting Act 1990, the appearance of candidates in programmes at the time of elections and the Representation of the People Act 1983.

## RADIO AUTHORITY ADVERTISING AND SPONSORSHIP CODE

Covers the presentation and standards for advertisements with appendices and also the guidelines on programme sponsorship.

All Radio Authority Codes can be obtained from the Radio Authority, Holbrook House, 14 Great Queen Street, Holborn, London WC2B 5DG, Tel 020 7430 2724. Their website is www.radioauthority.org.uk.

## BBC'S PRODUCER'S GUIDELINES

The BBC issues comprehensive guidelines for production personnel (easily accessed both in paper versions and on the Intranet) constantly updated to cover issues as and when they arrive. The Director General, Greg Dyke, who took office in 2000, has recently revised them. They cover issues from editorial policy, the use of children, quizzes and game shows, commercial relationships and programme funding. In effect, anything and everything to do with programme making and the decisions and ethical issues involved. Abridged versions are available for those who work in ITV or cable and satellite companies via the BBC website and they offer excellent guidance as to what is and isn't acceptable practice. The BBC considers its guidelines as more stringent than those of the ITC which means productions eventually transmitted on non-BBC stations also conform to the ITC. As many independent companies are commissioned by the BBC, those programme makers must also adhere to the BBC guidelines.

The BBC website is on www.bbc.co.uk and the website pages for the guidelines have an address starting www.bbc.co.uk/info/editorial/prodgl.

# Appendix 2
# Risk assessment and health and safety

The Health and Safety Executive Internet address is: www.hse.gov.uk and the following guidelines can be downloaded from there. Since writing, other directives may have been produced.

Facts for Freelances    www.hse.gov.uk/pubns/indg217.htm
Managing Crowds Safely    www.hse.gov.uk/pubns/indg142.htm
Safety in Broadcasting Sports Events    www.hse.gov.uk/pubns/etis1.htm
Smoke and Vapour Effects used in Entertainment    www.hse.gov.uk/pubns/etis3.htm
Violence to Workers in Broadcasting    www.hse.gov.uk/pubns/etis2.htm
Working with Animals in Entertainment    www.hse.gov.uk/pubns/etis4.htm

HSE Books has produced *Camera Operations on Location, Guidance for Managers and Camera Crews*, an indispensable booklet covering general risk assessment and safety whilst on location. It has an excellent checklist/memory aid on:

- the working environment;

- manual handling;

- electricity;

- general safety issues.

There is also a hazard checklist.

# HEALTH AND SAFETY ISSUES

## Further reading

*A Guide to the Health and Safety at Work etc. Act 1974*, 5th edn, HSE Books.
*A Guide to the Reporting of Injuries, Diseases and Dangerous Occurrences, Electrical Safety at Places of Entertainment*, GS 50, HSE Books.
*Essentials of Health and Safety at Work*, HSE Books, 1994.
*5 Steps to Risk Assessment*, IND(G)163L, HSE Books, 1994.
*Regulations*, L73, HSE Books, 1996.
Small, Robin, *Production Safety for Film, Television and Video*, Focal Press, 2000.

This is not an exhaustive list and obviously some of the books are more relevant to, say, electricians or location managers, but knowing the main regulations will certainly help – especially when you become a producer and are responsible and liable for the safety of your production personnel and crews.

# Appendix 3
## Organisations

BAPLA (British Association of Picture Libraries and Agencies) 18 Vine Hill, London EC1R 5DX, Tel 020 7713 1780. E-mail: bapla@bapla.demon.co.uk, website: www.bapla.org.uk.

BPI British Phonographic Industry Anti Piracy Unit, Elgar House, 41 Streatham High Road, London SW16 1ER, Tel 0181 664 4400.

Broadcasting Standards Commission, 7 The Sanctuary, London, SW1P 3JS, Tel 020 7808 1000, Website: www.bsc.org.uk.

The British Copyright Council, Copyright House, 29–33 Berners Street, London W1P 4AA, Tel 020 7359 1895.

British Film Commission (also for information about local film offices), 10 Little Portland Street, London W1W 7JG, Tel 020 7861 7860. Website: www.bfc.co.uk or www.britfilmcom.co.uk.

British Library, 96 Euston Road, London NW1 2DB, Tel 020 7412 7332, Readers Admissions, 020 7412 7794. Website: www.bl.uk, e-mail: reader-admissions@bl.uk. The newspapers are held at Colindale Avenue, London NW9.

British Universities Film and Video Council, 77 Well Street, London W1P 3RE, Tel 020 7393 1500. Website: www.bufvc.ac.uk. Researcher's Guide to British Film and TV Collections. This is mainly an academic source.

Celebrity Service Ltd, 93–97 Regent Street, London W1R 7TA, Tel 020 7439 9840. This service is not on-line yet but hopes *Celebrity Bulletin* will be from 2001.

Copyright Directorate, The Patent Office, Harmsworth House, 13–15 Bouverie Street, London EC4Y 8DP, Tel 020 7596 6566. Website: www.patent.gov.uk.

CLA: Copyright Licensing Agency, 90 Tottenham Court Road, London W1P 0LP, Tel 020 7436 5931. Website: www.cla.co.uk.

Equity, the actors' union: Guild House, Upper St Martins Lane, London WC2H 9EG, Tel 020 7379 6000. E-mail: equity@easynet.co.uk, website: www.equity.org.uk/equity.

Health and Safety Executive has several regional offices and the up-to-date numbers will be found in the phone directory: www.hse.gov.uk.

ITC Independent Television Commission: licenses and regulates independent television. There are several regional offices but the head office is ITC, 33 Foley Street, London W1W 7TH, Tel 020 7255 3000. Website www.itc.org.uk.

MCPS Mechanical-Copyright Protection Society, 29/33 Berners Street, London W1P 4AA, Tel 020 7580 5544. Website: www.mcps.co.uk.

MPA Music Publishers Association, 3rd Floor, Strandgate, 18–20 York Buildings, London WC2N 6JU, Tel 020 7839 7779.

MU Musicians Union, 60–62 Clapham Road, SW9 0JJ, Tel 020 7582 5566. Website: www.musiciansunion.org.uk.

The Patent Office, Concept House, Cardiff Road, Newport, Gwent NP10 8QQ, Tel 01645 500505.

The Personal Managers Association, Rivercroft, 1 Summer Road, East Molesey, Surrey KT8 9LX, Tel 020 8398 9796.

PPL Phonographic Performance Ltd, 1 Upper James Street, London W1R 3HG, Tel 020 7534 1000. Website www.ppluk.com.

Press Association News, PA News Centre, 292 Vauxhall Bridge Road, London SW1V 1AE, Tel 020 7963 7000/7146. Pictures: Tel 020 7963 7155. Website: www.pa.press.net. There are several regional offices.

PRS Performing Rights Society, 29/33 Berners Street, London W1P 4AA, Tel 020 7580 5544. Website: www.prs.co.uk.

PRO, Public Record Office, Kew, Richmond, Surrey, TW9 4DU, Tel 020 8876 3444. Website: www.pro.gov.uk.

Radio Authority, Holbrook House, 14 Great Queen Street, Holborn, London WC2B 5DG, Tel 020 7430 2724. Website: www.radioauthority.org.uk.

Society of Authors, 84 Drayton Gardens, London SW10 9SB, Tel 020 7373 6642. E-mail: authorsoc@writers.org.uk. Website: www.writers.org.uk/society.

Sport England, 16 Upper Woburn Place, London WC1H 0QP, Tel 020 7273 1500. Website: www.sportengland.org.

# Appendix 4
# Directories

*ASLIB Directory of Information Sources in the United Kingdom*, Reynard, Keith W. and Reynard, Jeremy M.E. (eds), very similar to the Directory of British Associations but also covers the subject range of the information held and the contact names. Also on CD Rom. Association for Information Management, Staple Hall, Stone House Court, London EC3A 7AB, Tel 020 7903 0000. Website: www.aslib.co.uk.

*Benn's Media Directory* comes in three volumes (UK, Europe and the rest of the world) and is expensive with (2000 price) one volume at £145. The most comprehensive directory with 17,000 media organisations, magazines, publications and broadcasting stations listed in the UK volume. Mainly lists to whom one sends press releases or buys advertising or for support organisations. *Benn's Media Directory*, Miller Freeman PLC, Riverbank House, Angel Lane, Tonbridge, Kent TN9 1SE, Tel 01732 362666.

*British Film Commission's Check Book*, information on all aspects of filming. The British Film Commission, 10 Little Portland Street, London W1W 7JG, Tel 020 7861 7860. Website: www.bfc.co.uk or www.britfilmcom.co.uk.

*BFI Film and Television Handbook* (published annually), British Film Commission, 10 Little Portland Street, London W1W 7JG, Tel 020 7861 7860.

*Civil Service Yearbook*, published twice and in 2000 the book, complete with CD Rom, cost £40. Lists main numbers and top personnel in Whitehall. Stationery Office, www.civil-service.co.uk.

*Directory of British Associations* lists associations in alphabetical order but with a subject index at the end. Indispensable. CBD Research Ltd, Beckenham, Kent.

*The Guardian Media Guide*, Peak, Steve and Fisher, Paul (eds) Fourth Estate, published annually. Almost indispensable

*Hansard*, published daily, records minutes from the proceedings at the House of Commons and is provided by subscription. Mainly for the newsroom, it is unlikely the general researcher would need access to this. Website: www.parliament.the-stationery-office.co.uk/pa/cm/cmhansrd.

*Key British Enterprises 2000* gives 'The essential facts about Britain's 50,000 leading businesses'. Includes principals (i.e. the directors and company secretaries) and sales figures; published in several volumes and on CD Rom. Very expensive, published by Dun and Bradstreet, Holmers Farm Way, High Wycombe, Buckinghamshire HP12 4UL, Tel 01494 423689.

*Kaye's Directory*, a production manual listing everything for the video, film and TV industry from accountants to wardrobe assistants. Kaye Media, Pinewood Studios, Pinewood Road, Iver Heath, Bucks SL0 0NH, Tel 01753 651171, subscription only.

*The Knowledge*, a directory and database for the film, TV and new media industries including companies, crews and contacts. Indispensable. Published by Miller Freeman PLC, Riverbank House, Angel Lane, Tonbridge, Kent TN9 1SE, Tel 01732 362666. www.theknowledgeonline.com.

*The Spotlight*, publishers of an actors' directory, 7 Leicester Place, London WC2 7BP, Tel 020 7437 5881. Website: www.spotlightcd.com.

*Whitaker's Almanack* is an annual collection of data on the UK plus more. The concise version includes: calendars, the peerage and lists, decorations, parliament and procedure, MPs and constituencies, government departments with dignitaries, civil service salaries, Forces lists and salaries, the Church of England, Roman Catholic Church and dignitaries, education and institutions including universities and independent schools plus fees, social welfare, the service industries, transport and communications, weights and measures, local government, major events of the previous year and obituaries. The hardback version has additional sections on finance, legal notes (including consumer law, wills, divorce, intellectual property), the media, organisations (including trade associations, trade unions, sports bodies and clubs), countries of the world (including exchange rates and time zones) and information about the previous year (including archaeology, broadcasting, the arts, and lists of acts and white papers). This is a must-have-access-to book in at least the concise version. *Whitaker's Almanack*, J. Whitaker and Sons Ltd, 12 Dyott Street, London WC1A 1DF. Website: www.whitakers-almanack.co.uk.

*The White Book*, a comprehensive source of specialist events contacts in this country and abroad for the music and event industry covering concert production and promotion, publicity and marketing, manufacturers, conference and exhibition industries from record companies, TV, film and video industries to artists, agents and managers. Less useful than *The Knowledge*, but still very helpful. *The White Book*, Bank House,

23 Warwick Road, Coventry CV1 2EW, Tel 024 7655 9658. Website: www.whitebook.co.uk.

*The Whitehall Companion* lists MPs and their constituencies, etc. In 2000, this book was £165 (see the *Civil Service Handbook* for a cheaper alternative). Published by The Stationery Office Ltd/Whitaker.

*Who's Who* (directory of influential people still living), published annually, A & C Black Ltd, 35 Bedford Row, London WC1R 4JH, Tel 020 7242 0946. Website: www.acblack.co.uk. *Who's Who* is not on the Internet but there is a subscription service via www.know.uk.co.uk.

*The Writers' and Artists' Yearbook*, A & C Black, published annually.

*The Writer's Handbook* (Barry Turner, ed.), Macmillan

For further listings of yearbooks and directories, refer to *The Media Guide*.

# Appendix 5
# Websites

No list can be exhaustive especially when new sites are coming on-line every day, so I have included all those I used for the book and others which should be of help. I have not listed the search engines.

192 (directory enquiries – not BT) www.192.com
British Association of Picture Libraries and Agencies (BAPLA) www.bapla.org.uk
BBC www.bbc.co.uk
British Film Commission www.bfc.co.uk or www.britfilmcom.co.uk
British Film Institute www.bfi.org.uk
British Library www.bl.uk
British Standards Commission www.bsc.org.uk
BT www.bt.com or directory enquiries service www.bt.com/phonenet.uk
BECTU www.bectu.org.uk
Clipsales, on-line archive service www.clipsalesnow.com
The Foreign Office www.fco.gov.uk/travel.
Government, UK www.open.gov.uk and parliament www.parliament.uk
*The Hollywood Reporter* (trade paper) www.hollywoodreporter.com
HSE www.hse.gov.uk
Internet Movie Database www.imdb.co.uk
ITC www.itc.org.uk
ITN Archive www.itnarchive.com or www.itn.co.uk
*The Knowledge* www.theknowledgeonline.com
MCPS www.mcps.co.uk
MPs and constituencies www.ukstate.com
MU (Musicians Union) www.musiciansunion.org.uk
NUJ www.gn.apc.org/media/nuj
PACT (Producers' Association) www.pact.co.uk
Parliament www.parliament.uk Hansard is www.parliament.the-stationery-office.co.uk/pa/cm/cmhansrd
Patent Office www.patent.gov.uk

Pathé News Film Library www.britishpathe.com
Press Association www.pressassociation.press.net
Produxion – TV industry Web guide www.produxion.com
PRS www.prs.co.uk
Radio Authority www.radioauthority.org.uk
The Spotlight (actors' directory) www.spotlightcd.com
Talking Yellow Pages (0800 600 900) or www.yell.co.uk
Waterstones (bookshop) www.waterstones.co.uk
*The Whitebook* www.whitebook.co.uk

Many of these have links to similar sites.

# Glossary

**AD**  Assistant director, there are up to three assistant directors on a large drama production, the 1st AD acting the same role as that performed by the floor manager in a television studio.

**A & R**  Artists and Repertoire, the department in a recording company which finds and looks after the careers of singers and groups.

**Ads**  advertisements or commercials.

**Ad lib**  off the cuff, unscripted remark.

**Agreements**  contracts stipulating conditions on the use of recorded music or actors, etc.

**AP**  Assistant producer or associate producer.

**As live**  pre-recording a programme as if it were live so that the first take is usually the one used. If there is a severe technical problem, the tape is rewound and taped over. Pre-recording usually takes place very shortly before transmission. A half-hour 'as live' production theoretically will be recorded in half an hour. There is no editing.

**Atmos**  atmosphere, background sound effects giving the impression of an environment.

**Autocue**  an electronic prompt device from which newsreaders and presenters read the script, other makes include Portaprompt and Teleprompter.

**BA**  Broadcast assistant (radio equivalent of TV's production assistant).

**BAC&S**  British Academy of Composers and Songwriters, Europe's leading composers' organisation.

**BECTU**  Broadcasting, Entertainment, Cinematograph and Theatre Union, one of the industry's trade unions.

**BCU**  big close up, a camera shot.

**Blonde**  colloquial term for a transportable light with a yellow lamp holder (see 'Lighting kit').

**BPI**  British Phonographic Industry, association of UK record companies.

**BSC**  Broadcasting Standards Commission.

**Buy-out clauses**  clauses in a contract of employment 'buying out' overtime by paying an overall fee for the job.

**C/A**  cut away, a camera shot, usually a close up where the sequence 'cuts away' from the master shot to telescope time or as explanation. For example, when something is being referred to, the viewer is shown it in close up.

**CAA**  Civil Aviation Authority.

**Call sheet**   an information sheet explaining where and when filming will take place so everyone knows where to go and when.

**Cam**   camera.

**Cans**   colloquial term for headphones originating from the era when the sound was so poor it was like 'hearing through tin cans'.

**Captions**   the names of contributors shown on screen but also includes opening titles and end credits and any other onscreen writing. Generated by caption or character generators colloquially referred to as a *capgen*.

**Carnet**   a transit certificate for equipment (like a passport).

**Chopper shots**   colloquial term for shots filmed from a helicopter.

**Clearance**   see copyright clearance.

**Clip**   short extract from a longer item, an excerpt.

**Clippings/cuttings**   press clippings or cuttings taken from newspapers.

**Copyright**   the ownership or the right to reproduce any artistic work such as a book, film, play, photography, or piece of music.

**Copyright clearance**   the means by which permission is sought for copyrighted material to be reproduced.

**Corporates/corporate videos**   non-broadcast products made by small independent production companies for training, staff information or for promotional purposes.

**CU**   close up, a camera shot.

**Cue**   pre-arranged signal to start.

**Cue light**   a small light in a voiceover or sound studio giving the cueing signal.

**Cue sheet**   the paperwork giving technical information and script for a programme or insert.

**Cume**   cumulative as in running order time, the total running time up to that point.

**DAT**   digital audio tape.

**Defence Advisory Notes – D-notices**   issued by the Defence, Press and Broadcasting Advisory Committee designed to advise the media that if they broadcast or publish certain information, it may damage national security.

**Dolly**   the wheeled device fixed to a camera in order to facilitate a tracking shot.

**Dry run**   rehearsal without the cameras.

**Dubbing**   putting sound on to film or tape *or* copying films or tapes from one format to another or to the same format.

**Duration**   the running time, actual length, of a programme or item.

**EDL**   edit decision list, the order in which a film is cut. Also called 'paper edit' or cutting order.

**Embargo**   a restriction on when information can be disclosed.

**ENG**   pronounced 'enj' or 'E.-N.-G.' depending on the station, electronic news gathering is a type of lightweight video camera and sound recording system.

**Estab shot**   establishing shot, usually a long shot wide shot, the first shot in a sequence to establish where the action is taking place.

**Flash fees**   payment for 'flashing' a photograph or picture on television, a royalty payment.

**Freelance**   self-employed and not on a permanent contract.

**Futures desk**   the desk filing stories for possible future coverage in a programme.

**Fx**   effects, as in sound effects or special effects.

**Genny**   short for the generator used for supplying electricity on location.

**Gv or gvs**   general view(s), a camera shot.

**Hand-held**   shots when a tripod is not used but the camera is often supported by the camera operator's shoulder. A bad hand-held shot is nicknamed 'wobblyscope'.

**Hand-held cams**   cameras light enough to be taken off the tripod and used 'hand-held', i.e. on the shoulder or held low down for tracking.

**HSE**   Health and Safety Executive, the governing body to regulate health and safety.

**IBA**   Independent Broadcasting Association, now replaced by the ITC (Independent Television Commission).

**In cue**   the first words of an insert, although it can be music (The 'out cue' are the last words).

**Independent producers**   small production houses outside the BBC or main ITV companies.

**Insert**   a short item (e.g. a live or a tape insert) to be inserted into a programme.

**Intro**   short for 'introduction', i.e. the intro at the beginning of a programme or before a new item. The 'outro' is at the end.

**ISDN**   Integrated Services over a Digital Network. A better and faster digital signal which can be used for both voice and non-voice data over the public telephone system. It does not have the crackle of standard telephone lines but, of course, is more expensive.

**ISM**   Incorporated Society of Musicians, professional association for performers, composers and teachers.

**ITC**   Independent Television Commission, the regulatory body for television, cable and satellite programmes in the UK.

**LE**   Light Entertainment, a non-serious programme such as a quiz, chat/game show, music programme or the department producing it.

**Lighting kit**   a basic lighting kit is two red heads and a blonde plus sun gun and accompanying gels and filters. The *red head* has a red fitting for the bulb and a *blonde* has a yellow fitting. The blonde gives a more powerful light. A *sun gun* is like a large hand-held battery-powered torch usually used for lighting up faces. The *gels* (short for gelatine) cover the lights to diffuse them or help with the colour balance of the local lighting situation. *Filters* are attached to the camera lens and also help with the colour balance or to give fx such as graduated colour, 'star burst' fx.

**Links**   inserts to join items, they can be either spoken by presenters to camera or short animated 'stings'.

**Listings**   a list of events, cinema, theatre, music – in other words, what's on where, including television, radio and satellite programmes. Listings magazines include *Radio Times* and *TV Times*.

**MARS**   Multimedia Archive Retrieval System, a system for playing music and videos electronically.

**MCPS**   Mechanical Copyright Protection Society Ltd, an agency collecting royalties on behalf of composers and publishers whenever their work is recorded.

**MCU**   Medium close up, a camera shot, often referred to as 'Head and Shoulders', used conventionally in interviews and for newsreaders.

**MEP**   Member of the European Parliament.

**Mic/mike**   microphone.

**Montage**    either a sequence of short shots usually cut to music or sfx *or* the actual cut of the film – in France, the *monteur* is the editor.

**Moral rights**    the right of an author of a work to keep the integrity of how it is used or seen.

**MU**    Musicians Union, a trade union representing musicians.

**Network**    nationwide. Programmes going out 'network' are going out all over the country.

**OB**    outside broadcast, a live or recorded programme made on location for large events, effectively a travelling studio.

**OOV**    out of vision, similar to voice over.

**OPCS**    Office of Population, Census and Surveys, commonly known as the Census Office.

**Out cue**    the last words of an insert, but can be music. Knowing what the last words are acts as a cue for the studio presenter to get ready to speak and a mic cue for the engineers.

**Outro**    'outro'duction, the last statement in a programme, opposite to intro.

**PA**    Production assistant, Press Association, a news agency or Public Address system.

**Packages**    in radio, pre-recorded edited inserts 'packaged' up and including links, music and actuality.

**PACT**    Producer's Alliance for Cinema and Television, the UK film and television trade's main professional organisation.

**PAMRA**    Performing Arts Media Rights Association, collects and distri-butes performance income to its members.

**Panning shots**    a pan is when the camera is fixed to the ground, i.e. on a tripod, but is swivelled, *panned* from left to right or right to left (see 'Tracking shots').

**Paper edit**    also known as edit decision list, EDL or cutting order, a list of shots put into order so that the editor has an idea of what he is to cut.

**P as Bs**    Programme as Broadcast, notes to show what music, length, film, etc., is included on the programme for future payment purposes, usually compiled by the BA or PA.

**Peds**    pedestal cameras, heavy cameras on wheels used in OBs and studios.

**POV**    point of view, a camera angle which is the point of view of the subject, as in low angle shots for a baby or dog.

**PPL**    Phonographic Performance Ltd, collecting society licensing broadcast and public performance of sound recording in the UK.

**Press release**    an information sheet about a special event sent to local TV and radio stations and newspaper offices in order to receive publicity. Also called news releases.

**Primary research**    basic first-hand research such as going on a recce, talking to people, phoning them up.

**PRO**    Public Record Office, at Kew, London, where the UK public records are stored.

**Promo**    short for 'promotion', a trailer for a forthcoming programme.

**PR**    public relations.

**PRS**    Performing Rights Society, collects royalties on behalf of music creators and publishers for public performance and broadcast.

**PSC**    portable single camera, video not film.

**Public liability**   insurance to cover accidents befalling the general public, e.g. if a passer-by falls over a tripod in a street.

**RA**   Radio Authority, the governing and licensing body for radio stations in the UK.

**Red head**   a type of portable light, see 'Lighting kit'.

**Recce**   short for 'reconnaissance', a visit to a potential location to check on filming suitability and conditions.

**Release forms**   forms signed by programme contributors indicating the permission to be filmed, edited and transmitted on television or radio.

**Royalties**   the payment to a copyright holder for the use of their work.

**Running order**   shortened to R/O, the items and timings of a programme listed in transmission (or recording) order. Running orders on daily programmes like the news are moveable feasts depending on the importance of items.

**Running time**   shortened to RT, the length of a programme or an insert.

**Run through**   a rehearsal.

**Rushes**   the unedited shots from a camera. In the States, they are called the 'dailies' because they are traditionally viewed at the start of each day before filming resumes. In the UK, film was 'rushed' to the lab for overnight processing and 'rushed' back for viewing the following day.

**SADIE**   a digital editing system.

**SB**   short for 'simultaneous broadcast', a broadcast transmitted simultaneously on radio and television, for instance the BBC Proms. It can also be broadcast simultaneously to or from abroad down an SB line.

**Scanner**   mobile OB truck containing the control rooms for production, vision and sound.

**Script**   the complete text of the programme or insert. A camera script includes all the camera shots and movements.

**Secondary research**   research taken second-hand from someone else's first-hand research, i.e. a newspaper report (see 'primary research').

**Segue**   (pronounced 'segway'), the running together of two items directly after each other without a pause or presenter's link, especially used for music when the transition between the two tracks should be smooth.

**Sfx**   sound effects or special effects.

**Simulrec**   simultaneous recording.

**SOT**   sound on tape.

**Sound bite**   short pithy phrase either on video or audio summing up a particular point of view. It can usually stand alone; e.g. Margaret Thatcher's 'The lady's not for turning'.

**Spark**   colloquial term for electrician.

**Stings and logos**   five-second graphic inserts to act as buffers and links and for dramatic effect.

**Stock shots**   short generic film clips, e.g. 'woods' or 'gardens' or 'the Blackpool Tower' bought in from a film library or in-house library.

**Stringer**   a freelance contributor paid by the item, often a journalist or cameraman based abroad where UK staff are not employed, although stringers do work in the UK.

**Synopsis**   a précis of the basic story line.

**Talkback**   a communication system from control room to studio floor.

**Talking head**    colloquial term for someone talking in vision. It is generally regarded that too many talking heads make poor television.

**Telerecording**    a system of recording programme output onto film.

**Time code**    electronic system of numbering each individual frame of video and used for accurate editing.

**Time code in vision**    by having the time code in vision on, for instance a VHS viewing copy, the researcher or director can view the video at home and organise a paper edit or edit decision list.

**Tracking shots**    the difference between a panning shot and a tracking shot is that, in tracking, the camera is physically moved (either on tracks or when the cameraman walks with the camera) from left to right or forwards or backwards. A camera moving from left to right or right to left is a *crab right* or a *crab left*.

**Trail/trailer**    a short 'advertisement' for a forthcoming programme, also called 'promo', short for promotion.

**Tranny**    transparency (photographic slide).

**Treatment**    how an idea will be worked for the programme.

**TS**    technical supervisor, the engineer in charge of the TV studio or OB.

**TX**    short for 'transmission', when the programme is broadcast.

**Viewing copy**    a copy, usually VHS, which can be viewed at home or in the office.

**V/O or voiceover**    as in narration, when the speaker cannot be seen. In radio, the narration may be over low-level music.

**Vox pop**    *vox populi*, 'voice of the people', a short composite recording of several people's views recorded in the street or other public place. Alan Whicker is generally regarded as the 'inventor' of the vox pop.

**VPL**    Video Performance Ltd, UK collection agency licensing the broadcast and public performance of music videos.

**Warm up/warm up man**    introduction and chat to the audience to relax them before recording. If there is no specially-employed warm up man to do this, the presenter, producer or floor manager will do it.

**Wild/wild track**    the recording of atmosphere, actuality or sound effects without picture. Also called buzz track or actuality.

**Wind-up**    visual signal to warn of the approaching end of the programme or contribution. The signal can either be the index finger rotating vertically or by a flashing cue light.

**Wrap**    either a short piece of actuality introduced and back announcement (back anno) 'wrapped around' by a vocal piece or 'it's a wrap' – basically, filming has finished, it's time to wrap up the equipment and leave.

# Index